George Dawson

Angling Talks

Being the Winter Talks on Summer Pastimes

George Dawson

Angling Talks
Being the Winter Talks on Summer Pastimes

ISBN/EAN: 9783337258634

Printed in Europe, USA, Canada, Australia, Japan

Cover: Foto ©Thomas Meinert / pixelio.de

More available books at **www.hansebooks.com**

ANGLING TALKS:

BEING THE

WINTER TALKS ON SUMMER PASTIMES.

CONTRIBUTED TO THE "FOREST AND STREAM"

BY GEORGE DAWSON.

NEW YORK:
FOREST AND STREAM PUBLISHING CO.
1883.

NOTE.

THE following chapters were written by Mr. Dawson subsequently to his retirement from the editorship of the *Albany Evening Journal* last September. The series was broken off by the author's lamented death in February.

The "Talks" attracted wide attention at the time of their publication in the angling columns of the *Forest and Stream*, and were received with very cordial appreciation. It is thought that their collection into the present more permanent form will prove acceptable.

As a political writer of conceded power, Mr. Dawson wielded a trenchant pen; when he turned from the conflict of parties to the praise of the favorite pastime of "simple wise men," his essays, limpid as the crystal streams, are aglow with the soft summer sunlight and melodious with the songs of birds. When angling was the theme, he wrote from a full heart and in closest sympathy with the scenes and pursuits described. These "Talks" are brimful of manly, wholesome sentiment; there is in them all not a particle of cant. Their sincerity and overflowing spirit at once win the reader, and he perforce shares the author's enthusiasm. The effect is magical, like that of the mimic players in Xenophon's *Memorabilia*: he who reads, if he be an angler, must go a-fishing; and if he be not, straightway then must he become one.

FOREST AND STREAM OFFICE, APRIL, 1883.

CONTENTS.

SIMPLE WISE MEN.

Dear solitary groves, where peace does dwell!
How willingly could I forever stay
Beneath the shade of your embracing greens,
Listening to the harmony of warbling birds,
Tuned with the gentle murmur of the streams.
                                        —*Rochester.*

I HAVE often had to assure my critical and incredulous friends that it is by no means all of fishing to fish. The appreciative angler, who has inherited or acquired the true spirit of the art is not alone happy while plying his vocation, but happy also in the recollection of what has been, and in the anticipation of what is to be. To him memory and hope are equally satisfying—the one luminous with the mellow sunshine of the recent past, and the other all aglow with the assured good cheer of the near future.

Nor is the pleasure derived from a review of the incidents of the last outing wholly or chiefly associated with its material results. "Casting" and "striking" and "killing" belong to the mere mechanism of the art. Its real fascination lies in what one sees and feels: in mountain and valley; in river and lake; in sunshine and shadow; in the exhilarating atmosphere and delectable odors of the virgin forest; in the music of singing birds and in the soothing monotone of running waters; in the hush of the night watches, and in the quiet and repose best found in the "solitary places" where anglers "most do congregate."

It strikes me like the sound of a trumpet to remember my fights with three-pound trout, five-pound bass or thirty-pound salmon, but I find intenser ecstacy when I recall the circumstances and surroundings of these material experiences, the transparent brook, whose ripples were rendered

dazzling as molten silver by the sunshine glints which fell
upon them through the ever-waving branches of the pine,
or birch, or hemlock which over-arched it like a benedic-
tion; the pellucid waters of river or lake, whose unruffled
surface trembled as fly and leader touched its placid bosom;
the deep pool, cast into deeper shadow by the giant boulders
near which the lordly salmon rests on his upward journey,
and the thousand other "things of beauty" which fill the eye
and ravish the senses while watching and waiting, and casting for a "rise."

These are the pictures most distinctly photographed upon
the memory of the appreciative angler, and which come up
most vividly before him when he looks back upon what has
been.

Many pleasures leave a sting behind them. Not so this
fascinating pastime. It is as harmless as it is invigorating,
and as healthful as it is harmless. There are many things
for which I am grateful, but for few things more than for
my passion for angling and the reasonable leisure always
vouchsafed me to gratify it.

I say "reasonable leisure," because the most of what time
I have given to angling has been abstracted from the grind-
ing pressure of a busy life. And the fact has, I am sure,
intensified my love for the pastime. As the dawn is most
gladly welcomed by the weary watcher who is waiting for
the morning, so a holiday brings most pleasure to those who
have earned it by hard work or patient service. The "cum-
berer of the ground," whose only employment is to "kill time"
and battle with *ennui*, has no holiday. He can no more appreciate the luxury of "a rest" than can the surfeited gour-
mand the luxury of an appetite. But with the busy man,
held to the tread-mill of active life through eleven of the
twelve months of the calendar year, it is not so. His holiday is to him what the open door is to the caged bird, the
opportunity coveted by the Psalmist, to "fly away and be
at rest," to "wander far off, and remain in the wilderness,"
(Psalm 55, 6-7). Because most of my holidays have been
thus wrenched from the ever whirling wheel of time, they

have brought to me more joy than "when oil and wine increaseth." And as my love of angling has grown with my years, so every recurring holiday has been more impatiently longed for and enjoyed. If all my days had been days of idleness, bringing with them neither conscious responsibility nor the pressure of duty, I might have lived as unprofitably and passed through life as wearily as the *ennuied* pet of fortune, whose indolence and incapacity are the only products of his inherited wealth, and, worst of all, I might never have known the delights of that man who finds pleasure in the silent woods and loves to go a-fishing.

In my immediate vicinage there are not a few beside myself who are fond of the angle—quiet men of gentle habit—simple wise men, as unostentatious as they are merry-hearted, and who carry about with them a clear conscience, a contented mind and the elements of perpetual youth. It is their custom to often "forgather" while waiting for the return of "the time of the singing of the birds," when it will be right to go a-fishing. Among them are men of divers profession —philosophers and educators, merchants and politicians, but not one among them all who would engage in any service, however remunerative or honorable, that would debar him from his annual outing, with rod and reel, for trout or salmon. These meetings are only less delightful than the fascinating pastime which constitutes the exhaustless theme of conversation. Every phase of the art is discussed, but the experiences of each individual during the just closed season is always first in order. Some of these experiences will enter into these familiar "Winter Talks on Summer Pastimes."

ABOUT BASS.

When time, which steals our years away,
  Shall steal our pleasures too,
The memory of the past will stay,
  And half our joy renew.   —*Moore.*

ABOUT BASS.

THE most highly esteemed member of our coterie devotes his leisure in angling for bass. He was born on the banks of the St. Lawrence, and before he had mastered his alphabet or shed his short-clothes he had become familiar with the haunts if not with the habits of this gamy fish. Indeed, although he has passed his three score years, his "memory runneth not to the contrary" when he would not rather fish than eat. The implements he used were primitive but effective—of just the form and calibre of those we often now see in the hands of our juvenile Waltons—less ornamental than useful, and intended not to "play" a fish but to "yank" him, with the least possible ceremony, from his aqueous element. It is not strange, therefore, that he is passionately fond of the pastime and as eager, now that "his hoary head is hid in snow," as when, "in the morn and liquid dew of youth," he gladly accepted the task of keeping the family table supplied with the results of his infantile labors.

There are few busier men in the marts of trade to-day and no man anywhere less likely, from habit or temperament, to squander either time or fortune. He never turns the back of his hand to a friend nor the back of his coat to an enemy, and would sooner lose the best customer on his long list than forego his visits to bass waters in July and October. I never knew a man with a more perfectly balanced double nature. As a merchant he is sedate, reticent and absorbed. As an angler he is cheerful, voluble and merry-hearted. Ten words suffice him to sell a hogshead of sugar, but he will talk an hour on the felicity of striking, fighting and killing a five-pound bass. I once asked him the weight of the largest fish he ever caught. His response was:

"I am not sure that I can answer your question. I caught what I believe to have been my largest bass when we never thought of weighing them. In my early days, when I fished with a hooppole and corresponding appendages, this thing happened to me: A rough dock extended a few feet out into the river in front of my father's farm. It was placed at a point in the river where the current flowed with moderate rapidity over a pebbly bottom. It was not merely just the kind of water bass take to in October, but its attractive qualities were augmented by the moss-covered logs which constituted the base of the rickety old dock from which I was wont to angle. On one memorable occasion—I could not have passed my tenth year—my hook was seized by the largest fish I had ever seen of the bass family. My line was not more than twelve feet in length, and it took my lusty visitor but an instant to run off with the slack and force the barb clean through his ponderous jaw. The result was a leap that made my hair stand on end, and brought me to my feet quicker than you could say 'Jack Robinson.' My first impulse was of course to 'yank' him, but I might as well have tried to 'yank' the dock itself from its moorings. Finding him bent on mischief, and foreseeing a long fight, I followed his lead and managed to get on the pebbly beach where I hoped to be able to take him out of the net. But, do my best I could not manage it by any of the processes with which I was familiar, and finding myself dragged toward a slough in which I would have been incontinently swamped if I had attempted to cross it, in sheer despair I made a bee line for the bushes, and very unartistically but very surely ran him ashore—the largest bass, by the common verdict, ever known to have been caught in those waters. I have since landed hundreds of large fish, scores of them running from seven to ten pounds, but none of them at all approximating the dimensions of this gamy monster. Making all due allowance for the exaggerations of dim distance and the fervid imagination of inexperienced youth, I have not a doubt now, and never had, that he weighed fully twelve pounds, avoirdupois. That was nearly fifty years ago," he said, with a sigh, "but the recollection of the incident is as fresh in my memory as any event of the last twelve month. But more than that, I attribute to the ecstasy which came to me from the capture of that fish the passion for angling which has grown with my years, and from which I have derived more real pleasure (to parody an old couplet) than

> ——'Any modern Cæsar feels
> With an obsequious Senate at his heels.' "

"I suppose," queried one of the party, "other fish than bass were abundant in those days?"

"Oh, yes! superabundant. Pickerel and muscalonge were 'plenty as blackberries.' But I never took to either. Pickerel were my especial boyhood abhorrence, and how any true 'brother of the angle' can so much as touch one of the slimy brutes is beyond my comprehension."

This remark was received with cordial approval, and fresh cigars all round. Not all present were veterans in the art, but none of them had the bad taste to call pickerel fishing a pastime. In commenting upon the subject, the veteran *par excellence* among us spoke thusly:

"No man ever fell in love with poetry by reading doggerel, nor did any one ever acquire a passion for angling by catching pickerel. It had been my habit from youth up to idle away an hour now and then fishing for perch, sunfish, bullpouts and low down trash of that sort. But I did that simply as an incident in my summer afternoon rambles by the lake shore and river side, and not because I cared a straw for or hankered after that kind of fishing; but once in my out-of-the way saunterings I fell in with a friend who was patiently whipping a trout brook. It was a real pleasure to recline beneath the shadow of a great rock and watch his graceful "casts." He had very few responses, but when a response came, the delight he evinced as he played and landed his four or eight ounce fish was fully shared by myself, and I soon found myself fascinated by what my friend was doing. The stream which ran through a beautiful valley, was cast into deep shadow by the graceful forest trees which lined its borders. Not a sound was heard, save a few bird-notes or the rustling of the leaves as they were moved by the gentle summer breeze which fanned them. The whole scene was a poem, and although I have been in just such places and passed through just such experiences a thousand times; this first picture of the first trout stream I ever saw, comes up before me as distinctly and as vividly as it presented itself to my vision forty years ago.

"Finding me thus interested in what he was doing, my friend, with the kindliness and generosity characteristic of the brotherhood, proffered me his rod for a cast. I timidly accepted his offer, and tried, very awkwardly, to do as he bade me. You can imagine with what success. He was an expert; I was a novice. He could cast fifty feet without an effort. When I essayed so much line as the length of the rod the fly came back upon me as if in derision. But I very soon succeeded in reaching the center of the stream, when there came a leap and a strike which made every nerve in my body quiver like a thrummed harp-string. I stood in motionless ecstacy for a moment, but, as I think, there came to me the inspiration of the born angler, for I played and landed that pound trout with the skill and judgment (my friend being witness) of a veteran. It was the largest trout known to have been taken from that stream in many years. That incident fixed my destiny. Until I had that experience fishing had no more attraction for me than any minor amusement with which we "kill time" when we find it a burden. From all of which I merely wish to say that no amount of pickerel or bull pout fishing could ever have inspired in me or in anyone the emotion needful to create the passion for such sort of angling as fascinates while it invigorates and augments the wisdom of the wise and makes

good men better. Such sort of angling inspires something
more than rod and line, 'with a worm at one end and a fool
at the other.' There must be rivulet and lake, forest and
mountain, sunshine and shadow, the music of birds, the melody of running waters, delicate tackling, and the rise and
strike and swirl of bass, trout or salmon. Where such
things are combined with the love of nature inherent in the
contemplative, mild-mannered and gentle disciples of the
historic fathers of the art, angling becomes an irresistible
fascination, and gives rest to the weary, vitality to the over
wrought, cheerfulness to the despondent, ambling rhythm
to the life that now is, and a clearer appreciation of the
promised felicities of the life that is to come."

A quiet ripple of applause greeted this rhapsody of the
honored mentor of the happy group, when our bass fisher
from the St. Lawrence was asked:

"Did you never hook a muscalonge?   They are certainly
a gamy fish, quite deserving the attention of the most fas-
tidious angler."

"Oh, yes; I have often taken muscalonge on a trawl, and
their capture gave me a great deal of muscular exercise, but
nothing else.   They hook themselves, and all that is required
of you is to drag them in, hand over hand, as rapidly as
possible.   It requires a little skill to get them in your boat
without upsetting, but not much more than to do the same
thing with a water-soaked log, and hauling them in is very
much like hauling in the same weight of deadwood against
the current.   Yes, I have caught muscalonge of all weights,
from five to thirty pounds, but I would rather take a five-
pound bass on an eight-ounce fly-rod than a score of muscalonge at the end of a two or three hundred feet trawl."

"How do the quantity and weight of bass in the St. Lawrence now compare with forty years ago?"

"I do not think the quantity has materially diminished,
but they have changed their haunts.   I find very few now
where they used to be abundant, and places where we never
had any luck in old times now teem with them.   They are
not nearly as plenty among the Thousand Islands as they

used to be, and no wonder. What with steam yachts and fishing boats, 'thick as autumnal leaves that strow the brooks in Vallombrosa,' and net and spear and indiscriminate slaughter, in season and out of season, by thousands of experts and amateur idlers, it is a marvel that the whole species was not long ago exterminated. And the weight of the fish has fallen off in even greater proportion at that point. The capture of a five-pound bass to-day is something to talk about; forty years ago bass of that weight uniformly made up one-fourth of my catch. The truth is, the fish haven't time to grow—with so many to beguile them, they are caught as soon as they can snap at a hook or rise to a fly. But there are still pleasant and prolific places in the St. Lawrence—I will name some of them to any of you in a whisper—where I never fail to take them as abundantly and of as great weight, with my eight-ounce rod and tiny fly, as I did forty years ago with my mammoth hoop-pole and ponderous tackling."

"But you do not now confine yourself to the St. Lawrence in your search for bass?" was the next query, not because we did not know, but simply to start him off on his favorite hobby and hear him expatiate upon the pleasant places to which he is beguiled during the season when it is right to go a-fishing.

"By no means," was his reply. "I find it true in angling as in everything else—'variety's the very spice of life.' With my love of the pastime has grown my love for, and appreciation of, the grand and beautiful in nature, and I have fished for bass in all waters, from the unbroken wilds of Canada to the primitive forests of Northern Michigan. The lakes where they most abound, wherever found, are invariably gems of transparent purity, and are almost as inviting to the appreciative eye because of their picturesque surroundings as because of what they hold for the angler. Wherever I have gone, whether to the remote North or to the far West, I have never failed to find what I went for, plenty fish, good sport, magnificent scenery, mental repose and physical recuperation. It is a pastime that gave moral fibre to the apostles and æsthetic delectation to the simple wise men of all ages."

To this, of course, all present gave cheerful response, as will all others who live virtuous lives and like to go a-fishing.

ABOUT GRAYLING.

Hide me, ye forests. in your coolest bow'rs,
Where flows the murmuring brook, inviting dreams,
Where bordering hazel overhangs the streams.
—*Gay*.

It so happens that no one of the local brotherhood, except myself, ever fished for grayling. All have frequently resolved to do so, but none of them have yet found leisure to put their resolve into execution. As the next best thing, they require of me an annual recital of my visits to grayling waters. I am nothing loth, of course. On the contrary, it is a great pleasure, only less enjoyable than the reality itself. My "talk" this year was on this wise:

"A few years ago the Au Sable was the most famous and best stocked grayling river in Northern Michigan. When I became acquainted with it, the fish were very abundant. In an hour's casting at almost any point, a sufficient number could be taken to surfeit any reasonable angler for a day. But, unfortunately, all anglers are not reasonable. While making ready for a few days' sojourn on the river, a party came in with a barrel of fish they had taken, and which they proposed to carry home with them. They may have had a thousand or more, and to secure that number of sizable fish they had probably killed four times as many. With the utmost care the whole lot would doubtless be nauseatingly stale before they reached their destination. The purpose of the party was well enough; for it is always commendable to remember the loved ones at home; but I never felt that I greatly complimented a friend by presenting him with a mess of stale fish; and, except under very favorable circumstances, all fish become stale, however carefully packed, that can only be eaten a week, more or less, after they are taken. Neither grayling, nor trout, nor salmon, are in full flavor if they have been so much as twenty-four hours out of water. Many an honest angler has lost caste with his friends because the promise to the ear has been broken to the palate. His praises were based upon the flavor when freshly caught; their judgment upon the flavor when eaten. The original flavor of salmon remains longer than that of either trout or grayling. But even salmon greatly deteriorate in two or three days, however carefully packed. Whenever I bring any of my salmon catch home with me, I see to it that they are kept constantly encased in fresh ice and that they are not exposed to anything above a frigid temperature until they are passed over into the hands of the cook. In this way I have sometimes enabled my friends to get a fair if not a perfect idea of the exquisite salmon flavor.

"Since I first visited the Au Sable it has fallen off in both the number and weight of its fish. But it still affords good sport to those who do not engage in the pastime simply to see how many fish they can kill. 'Catching to count' is a species of vandalism in which no honest angler will engage. Those who do, whatever they may call themselves, have the 'low down' spirit of the pot-hunter, although they may not have his dollar-and-cent cupidity.

"I remember a great many years ago, hearing one of a party of four boasting that they had, in two days, taken twenty-two hundred trout from the waters of 'Stony Clove,' in the Catskills, and I once saw a then famous judge 'scooping up' trout from the same waters with a bed-tick he had either bought, borrowed or stolen from one of the neighbors. No marvel that that once prolific stream is now comparatively barren. Scores upon scores of other streams have been similarly depleted in this State and elsewhere. But I am happy to know that this unsportsmanlike habit of 'catching to count' is now deemed 'more honored in the breach than in the observance'—thanks to the admonitions of the public press and the better education of the present generation of anglers.

"On my first visit to the Au Sable I took all the fish I

wished within a mile from camp. On my recent visit it took me a whole afternoon, casting over the same ground, to catch enough for supper and breakfast. I was told they were plenty as ever fifteen or twenty miles down stream, but I didn't care to make the journey. I preferred to work for what I caught, having long since ceased to find my highest pleasure in angling where neither skill nor patience is required to fill my creel."

"In what," I was asked, "do grayling, in their haunts and habits, differ from trout?"

"Their haunts are the same, in every material quality. That is, the Au Sable has every feature of a trout stream, in the clearness, flow and temperature of its water, and in its ripples, eddies and pools. To simply look at it, any expert would pronounce it as promising a trout stream as he ever saw. When I began to cast, I expected a rise from a trout rather than from a grayling; but often as I have fished the river I have never yet so much as seen a trout."

"How do you account for their absence?" was the next query.

"I have been frequently asked that question, but I have never been able to answer it, and the answer is all the more puzzling from the fact that the earlier settlers have a tradition (and some assume to speak from personal knowledge) that there was once trout in the river, and that even now there are both trout and grayling in other waters not far off. If the tradition is truthful in regard to this river, what has become of the trout? Have the grayling destroyed them? If so, how did it happen, after having dwelt together in unity since the creation, in these latter days 'the one has been taken and the other left?' I know that trout have disappeared from a great many streams because of the changed temperature or diminished supply of the water, caused by the artificial drainage of swamps, the absorption or diversion of springs and the denudation of forests. But no such causes have operated here. With isolated exceptions—few and far between—the swamps and springs and forests remain as they were when 'the morning stars sang together.'

If trout ever were in the river I can conceive of no reason why they should not be there still, and if in waters where the two fish are still found the trout are rapidly disappearing (as is alleged) the mystery is all the more inexplicable. I wish some one better acquainted with grayling and grayling waters than I am would essay to solve this problem.

"So much for the haunts of the grayling. Now a word about their habits. I find them in just such spots as I would look for trout in the early season—on the riffs, at the foot of rapids, under old logs and in all kinds of shady places, but not often in deep pools. And they are like trout also in the manner in which they take the fly, except that I thought they did not come up as far out of the water as trout sometimes do when they 'rise;' but they take the fly as sharply, shoot off as rapidly and fight as gamely. They make a more stout resistance at the outset than trout of the same weight, chiefly because of the great dimensions of their dorsal fin, which gives them a powerful lever when they shoot across the current, as they usually do when struck. I do not think, however, they have the trout's 'staying' qualities, but they are all game, and afford the angler quite as much sport as trout in any waters.

"There is one thing about the grayling especially worth mentioning—the peculiar thyme-like aroma they emit when taken. The ancient Greeks recognized this fragrant odor in the fish. 'Hence its generic name *Thymallus*, which is derived from *Thumallus*, the Greek term for thyme.' [Halleck's Gazetteer, p. 335.] I had never heard of this peculiarity, and for a time I fancied myself moving through a forest-garden of sweet smelling herbs. None of this aroma is perceptible after cooking—except to a very lively imagination. In point of flavor, the grayling is the peer of the trout. Indeed, neither in its haunts, its habits, its gamy qualities or its flavor, is it at all inferior to that favorite fish. If not as handsome when landed it is even more beautiful in the water. In reeling one in, with the sun at a proper angle, its great dorsal fin, with its blended body-hues of olive, brown, rose, blue, green and pink, reveal all the dazzling colors of the kaleidoscope. I am afraid I sometimes unnecessarily protracted my 'play' to enjoy the exquisite picture."

"You speak," said one of the coterie, "of the Au Sable as having the flow of an ordinary trout stream. The popular idea is that the whole of Michigan, except its extreme northern portion, is practically a uniform plane, with no high hills and no mountain brooks nor swift flowing waters, such as we have in our own State."

"And this popular idea is not far wrong. There are no real mountains in Michigan. Nevertheless, the topography of the center of the lower peninsula is such that many of the streams move with considerable velocity. The current of the Au Sable, for instance, flows from one to four miles an hour, and its water is as pure and as transparent as any mountain stream I ever saw. But when I have said this I have said about all that can be said in its favor. It has very few beautiful scenic features. Its banks are generally low and uninviting. There are not, so far as 1 traversed it, many pleasant camping places directly on its borders. On my last visit I floated several miles before I found a spot where I was willing to pitch my tent, and when I landed an incident occurred that made me wish myself a hundred miles away. It was this: A party of ladies and gentlemen had just broken camp as we landed, and were awaiting their wagons to take them to the village. While thus waiting, the ladies amused themselves in gathering wild flowers, and in their rambles they had encountered a huge massassaugua, whose glittering eyes and warning rattle had sent them flying and screaming back to camp. Although diligent search was made for the reptile. he remained undiscovered. The incident was followed by the pleasant assurance from my guide, that 'although a good many 'saugas were round, they very seldom bit anyone; or, if they did, a quart of whisky, swallowed at once, was a sure cure.' As I hadn't the whisky I didn't hanker after the bite. My sleep in the woods, with nothing but a few hemlock boughs between my body and mother earth, is usually sound and refreshing. But upon this occasion I was terribly nervous, and more than once awoke with the fancy that every hair on my head was a massassauga, and the rustling of the leaves the seductive music of their blood-curdling rattle. Fond as I was of fishing, before morning I had resolved that I wouldn't spend another such night for all the grayling in the Au Sable. But 'how use doth breed a habit in a man!' With the dawn my nervousness took flight, and through all the subsequent nights I spent upon the river, I 'slept the sleep of unconscious innocence.' Still, the knowledge that rattlers are occasionally seen has made me less anxious than I might otherwise be to go after grayling.

"It is one of the glories of the 'North Woods' that they are infested by no venomous reptiles; and during all the years I have visited salmon rivers, I have never seen nor heard of anything of kin to the rattlesnake family. I know of some splendid trout, bass and muscalonge waters northwest from Ottawa which I have hesitated about visiting because of their bad reputation in this respect. But even this will not restrain me through another summer, if my health is spared."

"When are grayling in season?" I was asked.

"The grayling is a spring spawner, and is in season anywhere from July to mid-winter. They are, perhaps, in fullest life and flavor in September and October, and thus furnish sport to the angler after it is wrong to take trout or salmon. In Michigan there is no more delightful month in the whole year than October. As a rule, it is an unbroken Indian summer, and as, late in the month, deer are in good flesh and are almost as plenty in the woods as grayling are in the water, a combination of the two makes the Au Sable region a very paradise to the sportsman. I may add, also, that there are lakes near by quite as well stocked with bass as the river is with grayling. A region where bass, grayling and deer are all 'in season' at once, and all equally abundant, should have a potent drawing power for all who take delight in the use of rod and rifle."

"Please take us with you the next time you go for grayling," was the expressed wish of all present—not excepting

my old friend from St. Lawrence, who had never before indicated any interest in any fish but his beloved bass.   I more
than half suspected, however, that his desire to accompany
me had its moving cause in my casual intimation that there
were inviting bass lakes in the neighborhood of this famous
grayling river.

A MEMORY.

How beautiful this night! the balmiest sigh
Which vernal zephyrs breathe in evening's ear
Were discord to the speaking quietude
That wraps this moveless scene.   —*Shelley.*

The casual presence of two or three out-of-town veterans
of the craft gave a retrospective cast to the conversation at a recent re-union of the local brotherhood. With
one of our guests I had tabernacled for twenty years in the
wilderness. No man was ever more companionable or had
more of the characteristics of true nobility. In physique
he was robust as an athlete, but in thought and feeling he
was as impressive as a child and as gentle as a woman. He
was, withal, as moderate in his sports as he was temperate
in his habits. In seeking his own pleasure he never forgot
the pleasure of others, nor did he ever envy others the
"luck" he sometimes failed to enjoy himself. Indeed, I
have known him to slip away from a promising "spring
hole" which was his own by right of possession, that a less
expert angler might fish undisturbed and be happy. He is
some years my senior, and although still as buoyant in
spirit as when he would "set the table in a roar" by the un-
ceasing flow of his inimitable humor, he bears, on body and
brow, the ear-marks of weariness, if not of decay. When I
meet him he always reminds me of my fancy picture of
grand old "Kit North"—that princely king of the inimitable "Noctes Ambrosianæ." He is like him in his tastes,
in his enthusiasm and in his irrepressible love of the gentle
pastime which constituted the rarest pleasure of his youth
and the chief joy of his green old age. He is like him also
in that he finds unalloyed delight in re-traversing, in imagi-

nation, the quiet places, where in his prime and later man-
hood, he was wont to go a-fishing.

And another of our guests was cast from the same mold.
He had, for.thirty years, without a single intermission, regularly visited the North Woods. He knew every foot of that
tangled wilderness; had fished in every accessible brook,
river and lake, and had never been known to do aught that
did not become an angler and a man. In all my long asso-
ciation with him, in town and forest, around the home-
hearth and the camp-fire, I never but once saw him out of
humor. The single exception was when a conceited cockney
—who had more of the spirit of the vandal than of the
gentle angler—happened along where we were in camp and
challenged him to a day's fishing to "count." Although
proverbially hospitable and never more happy than when
entertaining casual guests, he made his contempt for his
challenger so unmistakable that the fellow was glad to
"vamose the ranch" at the earliest possible moment. If all
other honorable anglers were equally emphatic in their de-
nunciation of this vile habit, our trout streams would not
be so soon depleted.

After all were comfortably seated around the open fire-
place, and our venerable guests and all of us were well down
to the middle of our first cigar, the oldest and most honored
of the circle said:

"Well, this is comfortable. This crackling wood fire, this
fragrant Havana (only it should be a pipe), and these friendly
and familiar faces have knocked thirty years of time into
oblivion and dropped me down into the cosy precincts of a
bark shanty at the foot of Big Tupper. Some of you
younger gentlemen were then still in your swaddling clothes,
but you and you and you [naming three of us] were there
or thereabouts years before and for many years thereafter.
Providence has dealt kindly with all of us. My own cruse
has never been without oil, and I never took physic enough
to nauseate a cat. In the beautifully expressive language
of Scripture, my 'lines have been cast in pleasant places.'
I never had an ailment a week's fishing wouldn't cure, and

I never envied prince, potentate or president so long as I
could find the time (and I always did) and had the opportu-
tunity to make a 'cast.' I think I am and have been as
sympathetic as most men. ["Hear, hear," all around the
circle.] I know I have lost many a night's sleep on hearing
of the misfortune of some friend who deserved a better
fate. I know, too, that I would rather toss a dollar to a
beggar than exchange salutations with a king, and I have
had both experiences. Indeed, my sympathies have uniformly been with 'the under dog in the fight,' no matter
which was the aggressor. But my heart has always been
stirred to its deepest depths when I have met a good fellow
who was so insensible to his own happiness, so absorbed in
his acquisition of wealth, and so inappreciative of the ex-
ample of the holy apostles as never to have cultivated a
taste for the angle. ["Hear, hear," and a gentle ripple of
applause.] Why, what is life? and what is the prime
object of living? In one respect 'life is a vapor'; but it is
something more. It embodies all the elements of an active
verb—to be, to do, to suffer (as little as possible) and to
enjoy (all you can). That is a condensed epitome of life, as
I understand it. And what is the object of living? Simply
to do good and be happy. The one is dependent upon the
other. They are inseparable and indivisible; and 'what
God has joined together let no man put asunder.' I know
that an old Scotch philosopher—and no class of philosophers
blend more hard sense with their incomprehensible meta-
physics—has said that the root of all happiness lies in 'a
clear conscience and open bowels.' So far as that aphorism
goes it is incontestably sound and profoundly sensible. But
there is a link missing. I insist that however clear and
clean one may keep his conscience, and however regularly
the complicated machinery of his 'fearfully and wonder-
fully made' system may do its office, it is impossible that he
should ever be qualified for the highest good or reach the
highest possible pinnacle of earthly felicity, unless he has
the contemplative mind, the gentle spirit, the poetic taste,
the quiet habit and the sturdy common sense of the man

who loves to go a-fishing. ["Bravo!" "Well put," with approving smiles and affirmative head-nods from all of us.] Now, you see, 1 know what I am talking about. I was ten years old before I killed a trout. If my early education had not been neglected I would have begun fishing at five. The loss of those five years have always been a source of regret to me, and 1 more than once questioned my father's kindness because, with all his own love for, and appreciation of, the sport, 'he kept his only son, myself, at home' during these five years, while he himself made his weekly excursions to the trout streams in our immediate neighborhood. I am told that during those five lost years I was delicate, morose, flippant and querulous. No wonder. My inher, ited angling blood was in rebellion against the cruel restraint imposed upon me. But with a *carte blanche* at ten to fish when and where I pleased, the whole mental and moral structure of my being was changed, and I became ductile, obedient and happy; and 1 have been fairly good and very happy ever since, but never so happy as when I have had a 'lodge in some vast wilderness,' through which course melodious trout brooks or roaring salmon rivers." [Applause.]

When fresh cigars were lit and the blazing fire replenished, our venerable friend was reminded that he had not yet told us about the pleasant time he had in his bark shanty at the foot of Big Tupper thirty years ago.

"Thank you for the reminder. Well, you see, no matter how fond one becomes of the woods in general, or how happy he may be wherever there are plenty fish and pleasant scenery, he will get a special fondness for some special spot, and will never deem his outing complete without paying it a visit. I always had several such pet places, and Cole's Point, at the foot of Big Tupper, was one of them. I came to like the spot not alone because of its pleasant surroundings—although that counted for something—but also because, within easy distance, there were some of the best casting places, during the early season, to be found anywhere in the woods, notably the Point itself, Peter's Rock and Lothrop's chopping. My acquaintance with these

localities began nearly forty years ago, when the regular
visitors to those waters could be counted upon your two
thumbs and eight fingers, and when you could float fifty
miles without meeting a white man or encountering a house.
There are now, I am told, a hundred places of entertain-
ment within the boundaries of the grand old forest where
we used to pitch our tents without fear of molestation from
cockney anglers or 'Murray's fools.' As I was saying, Cole's
Point was one of my favorite resorts. The occasion to
which my memory drifted just now was only distinguished from many another because of two or three incidents which rendered it especially memorable. I was accompanied by two of the most companionable fellows I ever
met. They were born anglers, and carried with them all
the scholarly tastes and joyousness of spirit characteristic of
the old masters of the art. Dull care never obtruded his ugly
visage within the precincts of their tabernacle. Although
they were masters of all the sciences, and had earned all the
titles at the disposal of all the schools, they were as free
from guile and ostentation as a true angler is from cruelty
or conceit. While we were in camp the moon was at her
full, so that the nights were as luminous as the early gloaming, and as serene and beautiful as the placid waters of the
great lake which stretched out illimitably before us. As we
sat in rapt ecstacy outside our primitive camp looking up
and out upon the unclouded sky, the silvery sheen of the
quiet waters and the rugged bluffs which loomed up in the
clear moonlight like giant warders at the portals of the lake,
no sound broke upon the ear save the low ripple of the tiny
rapids just below us, and the occasional whistle of some be-
lated wood-bird who had missed his mate. You know I
have been a world-wide wanderer. There is not a historic
painting, nor a chronicled statue, nor a noted palace, from
the Hudson to the Bosphorus, that I have not seen. I have
slept upon an Alpine glacier, have sat in wonderment and
awe beneath the ponderous dome of St. Peters, have looked
down from the belfry of St. Paul's, have traversed the
Rhine, have bowed my head at the entrance of the Golden

Gate, have wandered through the 'garden of the gods,' and taken in all the exquisite beauty and majestic grandeur of the Yosemite Valley, but my soul was never so thrilled as during these never-to-be-forgotten nights of ecstacy and beauty at the foot of Big Tupper, when, superadded to what I saw and felt, my two companions made the dense solitude vocal with 'the concord of sweet sounds,' breathed from cornet and flute, played with a sweetness and harmony which proved them as much the masters of those instruments as they were of Greek and belle-lettres and of rod and reel. Much that I have seen and enjoyed is forgotten, but this memory of thirty years ago remains as fresh and vivid as any pleasurable emotion that has come to me within the past fortnight. Oh, no; as our respected chronicler of the pleasures of our favorite pastime has said, 'it is not all of fishing to fish,' and he who thinks so has not yet learned the first letter in the alphabet of the true angler. [Ripples of applause.]

"Did some one ask me what sport we had? In those days it required more skill to keep from 'striking' than to get a 'rise.' If we only went to fish, we need not then to have penetrated into the heart of the forest to get what we went for. But fishing was but an incident then as always. The freedom, the rest, the recuperation, the ten thousand delights which come to mind and heart from mountain and river and lake and forest, infinitely more than the mere act of taking fish, constituted and still constitute the chief charm of these summer rambles. As my friend here has said before me, among the multitude of blessings vouchsafed me by a kind Providence, I count my passion for this delightful pastime as chief. If not a better, I am sure I have been a happier man, because, during all my long life, I have found pleasure in the woods and loved to go a-fishing." ["So say we, all of us," and a hearty hand-shake all round followed the rehearsal of this pleasant memory. It was the preface to many another like recital, which held the merry-hearted coterie together far into the "wee, sma' hours ayont the twal," and which I may make "of record" before "reeling up" these rambling "Talks on Summer Pastimes."]

REMINISCENCES.

I have written for lovers of the gentle art, and if this which I have written falls into other hands, let him who reads understand it is not for him.—*W. C. Prime.*

THESE "Talks" are written on the presumption that they will only be read by the "simple wise men" who can sympathize with their theme and who are in accord with their sentiments. To those who know nothing of the art or of its delightful possibilities, they will be "as sounding brass or tinkling cymbals." But to the mild-mannered and merry-hearted brotherhood they may have something of the music of forest birds and the melody of running waters.

Not only has every pastime its special attractions, but its votaries have their special reasons for the high estimate in which they hold it. Others may, but they never weary of talking about it. What is true of other pastimes is pre-eminently true of angling. No other affords so many incidents that it is a pleasure to remember and a greater pleasure to recount to appreciative and sympathizing listeners. The "memory" which formed the theme of my last "Talk" was followed by other reminiscences, one of which is subjoined.

Several years ago I found that I had not time to make my usual August trip to the North Woods; but I knew very well if I allowed the month to pass without enjoying a "cast" somewhere I would find my mental machinery sadly out of joint. I had tried it once and remembered the result. I cannot say that I suffered any real physical detriment, but I evinced neither good temper nor good manners (and they always hunt in couples) until the fever subsided with the close of the season.

And this is the experience of all anglers who have had a taste of the invigorating and exhilarating delights that come to those who have even passable skill with rod and reel. Perhaps something of this feeling may pass into the experience of those who have only felt the excitement incident to the capture of fish with the rougher implements of the craft. "Still-fishing" with bait, or trolling with "spoon" or minnow is better than no fishing, as " 'tis better to have loved and lost than never to have loved at all." But that sort of fishing never reaches to the dignity of a passion. The outing necessary to engage in it may be missed, but no great disappointment will be felt if circumstances compel a resort to some other mode of diversion. But with those who have long enjoyed the ecstasy of fly-casting it is not so. To be satisfying, their "vacation" must carry them to trout, bass, grayling or salmon waters. No other harmless or healthful recreation takes so strong a hold upon one's spirit or imagination, because there is no other which meets so fully the mental, physical and æsthetic demands of mind and heart. In following the brooks and rivers which wend their way through forest and mountain and valley, where solitude has her abode and where rustling leaves and singing birds and the rippling music of running waters fill the air with perpetual melody, the appreciative angler, "born so," as good old Izaak has it, finds mental repose, physical invigoration, "beauty for ashes, the oil of joy for mourning, and the garment of praise for the spirit of heaviness." It is because these qualities inhere in the pastime—are identical with and inseparable from it—that it is so irresistibly fascinating to its votaries. They can be proffered no substitute, because, like matchless beauty, "only itself can be its parallel."

On the occasion to which I have referred, my usual two weeks' visit to the "spring holes" between Ray Brook and Setting Pole Rapids, where I have had such sport as lifted me into the seventh heaven of delectation, was reduced to a three-days' sojourn where the whistle of the locomotive could be heard, and where, if need be, a telegraph message could reach me. It was, I thought, a pitiful substitute for my old-time free and easy swing in the grand old woods, where, for so many years, a score of good fellows constituted the sum total of intruders upon its then unbroken solitude. Ah, those were days to be remembered—when trout were plenty and anglers, few, when you could float from Martin's to Raquette Falls, and from Blue Mountain Lake to the Old Forge, in midsummer, as undisturbed by human companionship as if you were a-straddle of the highest peak of the Rocky Mountains, when there wasn't so much as a log shanty on the whole line of the Fulton range or (with one exception)from Bartlett's away down to Downie's Landing. Most of the good fellows whom I was wont to meet in those far-back summer rambles have made their last "cast," and are now, I trust, enjoying infinitely higher felicity on the banks of that "pure river of water, clear as crystal," so graphically portrayed by the lonely seer upon the Isle of Patmos. Some of them—alas! how few—still remain to illustrate the beneficent influence of the gentle art upon the mind and heart and physique of its happy brotherhood. Here is a note just received from one of them. Although to him the grasshopper may have become a burden, the golden bowl is not yet broken, nor has his good right arm yet lost its cunning. His heart still pulsates with good will to all men, especially to those who "deal justly, walk humbly," and love to go a-fishing. He has the gentle spirit of the dear old masters, and whether, hereafter, his annual visits shall be many or few to the pleasant places where he has for thirty years found retirement, recreation, repose, and a higher conception of the munificence and loving kindness of the Heavenly Father, the recollection of his friendly courtesies and quiet ways will ever be a pleasant memory to those who have often met him in the woods and enjoyed his kindly hospitality:

"Keeseville, Essex Co., N. Y., November 27, 1882.
"*My dear D.:*

"I desire to express to you the satisfaction and pleasure already received from reading the two articles from your pen published in Forest and Stream. I trust they will be continued through all the bleak months of our weary winter. May I ask you, before you 'reel up,' to give us a 'Talk' on the dear old North Woods of the Saranac region and thereabouts? I very often recall the many times we have met there, and they are hallowed in memory. Last spring's trip made my thirtieth annual pilgrimage to those blessed haunts, but not with my usual enthusiasm. I miss old friends like yourself. As you can readily imagine, many changes have occurred in thirty years, and of many who were once our forest companions, 'there only remains to us,' as you have said elsewhere, 'the recollection of their pleasant ways and joyous companionship.' It makes me sad to remember how many have passed away with whom I have taken 'sweet counsel' in the dear old woods, but whom I will see no more this side the dark river.   Yours, very truly,   J. R. R.''

With but three days at my certain disposal, Manchester and its adjacent waters seemed the most available. I had heard of the pleasant valley through which clear streams meandered, and I found it all it was claimed to be, "beautiful for situation," and a very paradise in itself and in its surroundings. If I had had no other purpose than to fish, I need not have left the valley. I filled my creel as quickly as I desired. The weather was superb, the water was in prime condition, the responses were prompt, and the weight of the fish and their gamey qualities even more inspiriting than their numbers. But I wished to explore as well as to angle; to fill my lungs with the pure ozone of the mountains, as well as to fill my creel with the speckled denizens of the pearly brooks; to camp out, if but for a night, as well as to fish. I had heard of a tiny lake perched upon the summit of an adjacent mountain many hundreds of feet above the valley, difficult of access, as retired as any peak in the Coloradoes, and well stocked with large trout always available to those who had the skill to catch them. I was prompt to avail myself of the proffer of an escort thither, and in the early gloaming I found myself casting in vain for a rise. At the end of a half hour the full moon came up over the tree tops. As the unclouded rays fell upon the fair bosom of the ruffled waters, I realized something of what Tennyson meant when he wrote of "the shimmering glimpses of a stream." The tiny waves looked like rippling rolls of molten silver, and when the moon had reached an elevation where her beams could flash full upon the face of the forest-bordered lakelet, it made up a picture which has remained with me through all these intervening years. It was for this and such as this, equally as for the delight afforded by the pastime itself, that I had always made my semi-annual visits to the quiet places where trout and contemplative anglers are pleased to forgather.

But this beautiful picture, gorgeous and fascinating as it was, did not fill full the measure of my desire and expectation. While I had been casting and watching the silent march of "the silver empress of the night," the fire had been kindled, the pork had been sliced, and the frying pan stood ready to do its office, but no trout had been taken. The idea of going supperless to bed was not pleasant. The long tramp and keen mountain air had given me an appetite more biting than the chilly atmosphere with which we were environed. I had resolved to retire discomfited after another cast when I bethought me that what the scarlet ibis and brown hackle had failed to accomplish, might, under the favorable conditions of the hour, be effected by a well-poised dusty miller; and I was not mistaken. The first cast was followed by a rise. In five minutes a two-pound trout was ready for dissection, and in twenty minutes, eight others, aggregating nine pounds, had been taken in out of the wet, wherewith I was content and reeled up for the night.

The repast that followed was fragrant, luscious and abundant—such a feast as always comes to an honest angler when "good digestion waits on appetite." I cannot, however, say as much for my night's repose. A hastily constructed brush canopy sufficiently protected us from the fast-falling dew, and a thick layer of hemlock boughs—emitting an aroma as fragrant as the fabled nectar of the gods—was such a couch as kings might envy. When thus disposed sleep always comes to me without wooing, and it would have done so on this occasion but that my inexperienced companion, who had never before camped out, chattered so incessantly that I sought revenge by reciting every blood-curdling story I had ever heard or could invent about the mortal peril that besets whoever has the temerity to invade the haunts of venomous reptiles or ravenous beasts. The brief intervals of silence were broken by mysterious sounds, which I knew to be caused by the flight of prowling night birds, the gnawing and scratching of hungry grubs, or the

stealthy tread of fox or rabbit, but which he, in his nervous
excitability, magnified into the unpleasant proximity of
bear or wild cat. His frequently repeated "Hist!" "What's
that!" had become monotonous, and I was passing off into
peaceful slumber when I was startled by a yell from my
timid friend which could only have been born of genuine
fright induced by actual contact with some tangible object.
If his alarm was not justified it was excusable, for our
couch had been invaded by a prowling woodchuck, who
had been attracted by the fragrance of the discarded frag-
ments of our evening feast. This intrusion (when the in-
truder took flight, for he stood not upon the order of his
going, but went at once) was followed by profound silence
on the part of my friend and by blissful unconsciousness
on my own part, until a full chorus of forest minstrels and
the slanting rays of the morning sun admonished me that it
was time to try the virtue of a morning cast.

And I cast, but nothing came of it. There was not a ripple on the surface of the water, and as far as I could reach
it seemed like casting upon a floor of glass. Every moment
the sun glare was extending, and before I had become entirely hopeless of a rise, the whole lake shone like a great
mass of burnished silver. I was soon encouraged, however,
by a "break" some hundred feet beyond my cast. As there
was neither boat nor raft available, the "break" might as
well have been a hundred miles away as where it was. I
did my best to entice the sportive brutes shoreward, but it
was like "calling spirits from the vasty deep,"—they
wouldn't come. The more I cast the more they jumped,
but always at an unapproachable distance. Of course it was
provoking, and of course I looked about for some mode by
which I could circumvent and turn the tables upon my
sportive tantalizers. I discovered near by two dry logs—
barely two—which, if properly joined together, would suffice to bear me up if carefully manipulated. Withes were
procured, hastily twisted and used in the conventional way
known to all old woodsmen. A few minutes sufficed to
finish the work after a fashion, and while the fish were still

"making the water boil" with their sportive antics, my fly dropped in the very center of their circle, and was taken before it had fairly touched the water. The movement of fisher and fish was spontaneous. But the fish had the advantage. The lake gave him "scope and verge enough" to do his best, while I stood poised upon a structure so frail that its dislocation and engulfment was threatened by the slightest motion. To play the fish was not so difficult, but how to land him without toppling over was a problem whose solution troubled me not a little. But it was accomplished —not once, but many times in quick succession. If conscience makes cowards of us all, impunity often makes us inexcusably presumptuous. My good luck had this effect upon myself, and while playing what afterward proved to be a two-pound trout, I found the two sticks which formed my raft slowly diverging. Here was a dilemma. It wouldn't do to drop my rod and risk the loss of my fish; nor would it do to allow either log to take its departure without an effort to prevent it. I soon discovered that one of the withes had broken, and my only hope was to use my feet to hold the raft together until I could finish my fight and paddle ashore. But my efforts in this direction rather tended to widen the breach than close it, and while my fish was at his best I found myself in the attitude of the Colossus of Rhodes or the American eagle, who stood with one foot on the Pacific and the other on the Atlantic while he dipped his beak in the majestic Mississippi. My straddle was simply prodigious, and it continued to broaden with ever-increasing momentum until my feet seemed as remote from each other as the Hebrides from the Rocky Mountains. There was, in short, a great gulf between them, and I was rather pleased than otherwise when I found them once more brought into close proximity and rendering me useful service in my efforts to swim ashore—which, in this instance, I found to be even more easy than "rolling off a log." But during all these novel experiences and unexpected mishaps the "ruling passion" did not forsake me. I may not have been able all the time to keep a "taut line" upon my fish, but I held my rod, and so soon as I could touch bottom I resumed the fight and landed my two-pound trout as coolly as if nothing out of the ordinary had happened since he rose to my fly.

A rousing fire and a luscious breakfast soon put everything to rights; and with a better constructed raft and a keener zest for the sport, I resumed my fishing, and in an hour or two had a full creel with which to replenish the larder of friends in waiting at the foot of the mountain.

ABOUT SOME OF THE DISTINGUISHED ANGLERS OF OUR TIME.

> Though he in all the people's eyes seemed great,
> Yet greater he appeared in his retreat.
>
> —*Sir J. Denham.*

In the long catalogue of honorable anglers are the names of apostles, kings, princes, priests, poets, bishops, statesmen and philosophers—men who made history, ruled nations, honored the church, dignified humanity, and left the impress of their scholarship upon all the centuries. And what they did they did all the better—more wisely, more humanely, and with a higher conception of the sacred character of the work assigned them—because they had the contemplative habit, proverbial patience and gentle spirit of the simple wise men who love to go a-fishing.

It has been my fortune to know and to have "camped out" with some of the well-known men of our own time, and I have always found them as companionable and merry-hearted as the most humble of the brotherhood. If there was any difference in the zest and enthusiasm with which each class plied their vocation, it arose from the fact that to the former the pastime was in greater contrast with the social and official conventionalities which held them more closely in their chafing trammels, and so gave them a keener appreciation of the freedom which came to them in the quiet places to which their love of angling led them. To all such an "outing" was not simply a holiday; it was the unlocking of their official prison house; the lifting of a leaden weight from their weary brain; a translation from work and worry to needed rest and absolute freedom and repose. The contrast between what they endured and what they enjoyed—between the red-tape technicalities of official life and the rollicking abandon permissible in the cosy camp on trout stream or salmon river—is the contrast between purgatory and paradise; and when the rebound comes it is felt in every cell of the brain, in every fibre of the body and in every pulsation of the heart. I knew just how a Chief Justice felt when, coming in from our salmon pools to lunch, he cast himself at full length beneath the welcome shade of a spreading pine, with face aglow and his voice tremulous with devout thanksgiving and exclaimed:

" 'Begone, my cares, I give ye to the winds.'

"Ah! old man, old man, this indeed is rest."

"Yes, my dear fellow, it is pleasant and—jolly," was my response, as I ripped off a piece of fresh hemlock bark to serve as a table for our humble repast.

These ripples of ecstacy; these indefinable heart-zephyrs; these foretastes of a higher felicity, which drop into the soul like golden sun-glints through the quivering leaves of the waving forests, are among the unpurchasable luxuries of the appreciative angler, and come to no other in such full measure.

Vice-President Wheeler is one of the distinguished anglers of our own time. His visits to the Saranacs and adjacent waters were and still are as regular as the seasons. His home is in close proximity to the best fishing grounds in the State, and he has grown up as familiar with all of them as he is with the various rooms in his own domicile. He has been a member of our State Legislature, has repeatedly served his district in the House of Representatives, been Vice-President of the United States, and a busy man always, but he has never intermitted his annual visits to the beautiful lakes which make a terrestrial paradise of the far-famed Adirondacks. When, years ago, he was talked of for the high position which he subsequently filled, I ventured the prediction that he would take no office that would pre-clude him from these annual visits to angling waters. In 18:6 "Hayes and Wheeler" were the candidates of their party, and I was proclaimed a false prophet. But I not only knew my man, but the fascinating pastime of which he was a votary, and the result vindicated my prediction. He more than once mysteriously disappeared from his place as presiding officer of the Senate, and while others were guess-ing his whereabouts, his more intimate friends knew he had gone a-fishing. His robes of place were laid aside for the garb of the angler, and the restraints and formalities of his office for the quiet and freedom which can be found nowhere so perfectly as in the primitive forests and on the crystal lakes and flowing rivers where the veteran angler finds his most refreshing rest and highest delectation.

Although the ex-Vice-President is as skilled in all the mysteries of the craft as he is in all the intricacies of the civil law, and with all the profoundest principles of states-manship, he affects the troll rather than the fly, and is oftener seen leisurely floating over the silvery surface of the beautiful lakes than casting in either brook or river. While this mode of angling does not come up to the highest standard of the art, and fails to satisfy the more ardent, robust and enthusiastic of the brotherhood, it is full of attraction and affords supreme delight to the more repose-ful and contemplative. Indeed, the most enthusiastic of the craft—even those who fancy they would soon weary of the sport if they could not "cast" for their prey—are often lured by the pleasure available to those who spend the sunny summer days casting along the picturesque shores and among the fairy-like islands of our charming inland waters. Every measure of the oar reveals some new bit of landscape to be admired. Sunshine and shadow are ever busy painting pictures of ever-varying beauty. The gentle summer zephyrs float down from the forest-crowned moun-tains like heavenly benedictions. The balmy air, as free from the germs of disease and the odors of decay as the mind of the angler is from strife and contention, fills his

lungs as full of invigorating elixir as his heart is of grati-
tude and good will. Those who have felt all this—and all
of us have—will not think the less of our distinguished
fellow citizen because he mostly angles with the troll, and
seeks his pleasure and recreation in moving to and fro upon
the lakes, which sit like sparkling gems among the everlast-
ing hills of the far-famed Adirondacks. I hope, when my
right hand shall forget its cunning, and when from old age
or decrepitude I shall have fought my last battle on salmon
waters, to be able to glide gently toward the dark river in
the quiet and peaceful and happy way in which my honored
friend has so long found his highest pleasure and most
perfect repose.

Gen. Arthur, now President of the United States, is also a
well known "brother of the angle." He has all the best
qualities of the most famous disciples of the gentle art. He
is patient, courteous, companionable, enthusisastic and
expert. He is, withal, an ardent lover of all that is grand
and beautiful and picturesque in nature. As I have said of
another I can say of him, in all that moves our sensibilities
and kindliest sympathies he is as impressible as a child and
as gentle as a woman. In spite of the rough school in which
he has been a life-long pupil, his heart is "open as day to
melting charity," and his poetic tastes enable him always
and everywhere, to see

"Sermons in stones, books in running brooks,
And good in everything."

His love of the art is the outgrowth of his æsthetic sus-
ceptibilities, and this love will remain with him long after
the dazzling glories of office shall have lost their charm, because the beauties of nature are as varied and exhaustless as
the munificence and majesty of their beneficent author.
The pleasurable emotions they excite, like the eternal prin-
ciple mysteriously linked to our finite humanity, never die.
Than Gen. Arthur no man can pitch a tent more quickly,
adorn a camp more tastefully, cast a fly more deftly, fight a
salmon more artistically or bring him to gaff more gracefully.
I owe to his courtesy the opportunity to kill my first salmon,

have been with him in every phase of an angler's experience,
and know him to be the peer of the most accomplished and
most appreciative of the masters of the art. It has been his
good fortune to kill the largest salmon ever taken with a fly
on this continent; and it was because I knew his intense
fondness for the pastime that I appreciated how deeply he
felt his disappointment when, after his nomination as Vice-
President, I tendered him my congratulations, he said: "I
thank you, of course, but I am afraid that, for this summer
at least, it will keep me away from our grand old river." A
pastime that could be remembered and spoken of under
such circumstances must have a strong hold upon one's
affections. I am sure he looks forward hopefully to the day
when, relieved of the cares of his high office, he will be once
more permitted to pitch his tent upon the Restigouche or
Cascapedia and angle for salmon.

Gen. Spinner, ex-United States Treasurer, an octogenarian
with whom old Time has dealt very gently, and whose sign
manual is a type of his robust integrity and sturdy patriotism, is also one of the brotherhood. Long before his home
friends sent him to Congress or President Lincoln made him
the custodian of the treasury chest of the nation, he had become intimate with the best angling waters of Northern
New York. With him the pastime was a delight, less because of the fish to be taken than because of the pleasant
places to which their capture led him. He was a born
botanist as well as a born angler, and during his later years
he was quite as happy gathering the rare plants and ferns
and flowers he met with in his forest walks as in catching
trout. I have journeyed with him through the whole length
and breadth of our Northern forest, and I never journeyed
with a more happy or entertaining companion. While in
Washington through the terrible years of the war, he found
needed rest in frequent rambles along the Potomac gathering
flowers and angling for bass. His office, from which he
distributed thousands of millions of dollars without the loss
of a farthing, was a perfect museum of floral and botanical
specimens and of all the paraphernalia which go to make up

an angler's kit.   And now, at his home in Florida, although
he long ago passed the alloted life of man, the same habits
remain with him and the same pleasures come to him from
these cherished pastimes of his earlier years.   He would, perhaps, all the same have illustrated in his life the virtues of
an honest man if Providence had not, in addition to a vigorous constitution, given him the temperament and taste of an
angler, but the fact that he is an angler we may be sure
abstracts nothing from the high qualities which enter into
the mental and moral structure of an honest man.   May he
yet live many years to fish with leaders as tough as his constitution, and with rods as elastic as his humor and as stable
as his fame.

Judge Edmunds, the distinguished Senator from Vermont,
has been for many years a regular visitor to salmon
waters.   He has fished many of the best rivers of the Provinces, and is as expert as he is enthusiastic in the practice of
the art.   Of late years his daughters have accompanied him
and shared with him the great pleasure to be derived from
these annual visits to the quiet places where salmon and sea-
trout gather in their season for the delectation of the angler.
One of his daughters was long an invalid, and although she
was temporarily benefited by these summer sojourns in the
silent woods, she recently "entered into rest."   Hereafter
the pleasure the honored statesman may derive from his
angling excursions will be hallowed by the memory of the
heart-gladdening companionship of the "loved and lost."

Judge Folger, the present Secretary of the Treasury, is
also fond of the angle.   A coterie of genial gentlemen have
lodges on the banks of Geneva Lake.   The Judge is chief
among them in skill and enthusiasm.   He has been hoping
for years to accompany Judge Hadley, his near neighbor
and intimate friend, in his annual raid upon the king of
fishes; but he has always had the misfortune to be so tied
down by the galling withes of public responsibilities that
he has never been able to pass beyond the metes and bounds
of his official parish for the length of time needful to make
the trip and enjoy the longed-for luxury.   A seat will be

reserved for him in our cosy tent until a kind Providence shall enable him, unhampered by any special obligation to an exacting public, to try his 'prentice hand on the lordly salmon.

Although Gov. Seymour may not be technically classed among the brotherhood, he has the simple habits and æsthetic tastes of the contemplative angler. No one has a nicer appreciation of the beauty and grandeur of forest scenery, or of the beneficent influence upon mind and heart and body of an occasional sojourn in the silent woods. It is a rare pleasure to listen to his graphic descriptions of what he has seen and felt and enjoyed during his rambles in the Adirondacks. Unlike most of the visitors to that picturesque region, he was most charmed by his winter excursions, when the solitude of the woods was doubly solitary, and when the mid-winter camp-fire gave an aspect to all its surroundings as weird-like as it was fascinating. "You ought to go to the woods in mid-winter," he said to me or one occasion. "You will never have seen them in their sublimest grandeur and magnificence until you do." The very last conversation I had with him was on the always interesting subject to the angler of fish food, and the reasons why some streams are so much more prolific than others. His theory is the existence of a weed which attracts to itself and holds, if it does not produce, a species of insect or animalculæ of which fish, especially trout, are fond, and upon which they thrive. This weed can, he believes, be transplanted and should be introduced into all waters where trout are found. A treatise from his pen on this subject would be an important and valuable addition to the multitude of papers on practical themes which he has written. As one of our honored fish commissioners, such a treatise would come within his official province, and form an important addition to our piscatorial literature. Who will say what influence this love of the silent woods and the peaceful repose of rural life has had in moulding and developing the social virtues and pure public character of this unique and distinguished statesman? None of our public men have lived more circumspectly. His declining sun reflects a mellow light and will set in unclouded lustre.

Chief Justice Ritchie of New Brunswick, and Chief Justice Gray of Massachusetts (now of the Supreme Court of the United States), were two of the merriest men I ever met on angling waters. The former, though venerable in years, had all the ardor and enthusiasm of lusty youth, and was one of the most persistent anglers I ever encountered. He cast with the skill of an expert and fought his fish with a dash and impetuosity as exciting as it was masterful. Chief Justice Gray, with less experience and more deliberation in casting and killing, was like his brother chief in his intense love of the sport and in appreciation of the enjoyable possibilities of camp life on salmon waters. Among the picturesque memories of these two eminent jurists which remain with me is this: Chief Justice Ritchie had struck a large fish about the going down of the sun. Failing to return to camp before dark, his brother chief became alarmed lest some mishap had befallen him. Whereupon he hastily extemporized a number of birch-bark torches, and started out to the rescue. The lost chief was found enveloped in darkness, sturdily fighting a huge fish among rocks and rapids as impetuously and as resolutely as if the chances were not ten to one that at any moment his canoe would be wrecked upon some one of the hundred boulders which made the rapids directly below the pool in which he had hooked his fish a boiling cauldron. As Chief Gray approached him with his flaming flambeaux, the happy angler, in a voice which overtopped the thundering of the rushing rapids, in reply to the query, "What can we do for you?" exclaimed:

"Give me but light, Ajax asks no more,"

and, amid the ringing cheers of his admiring rescuers, after a further half hour's struggle, a thirty-pound salmon was gaffed, and these two jolly jurists, assisted by their equally excited guides, proceeded to camp—Judge Gray leading as corps commander of the most unique torchlight procession that ever gave escort to a conquering hero on land or water.

The unusual length of this rambling "Talk" prevents me

from referring to several noted churchmen and scholars with whom I have either camped or met in my forest tramps. Prominently in my mind as I write is an eminent and beloved Bishop, whose fondness for the pastime often leads him to the silent woods and crystal trout streams within easy reach of his cathedral parish. His appreciation of the dignity as well as of the churchly and fascinating character of the art may be inferred from the fact that he deems it no disparagement to his sacred office to be seen bearing with him homeward his well-filled creel and the tidy fly-rod which had been his only companion through the long summer's day. If any cavil at this apostolic habit of the reverend bishop, I would say to them as good old Izaak said to similar stupid critics of his own day: "Indeed, my friend, you will find angling to be like the virtue of humility, which has a calmness of spirit and a world of other blessings attending upon it."

ABOUT SALMON FISHING.

All things by experience
Are most improved: then sedulously think
To 'meliorate thy stock; no way or rule　·
Be unassay'd.　　　　　—*John Phillips.*

I AM often questioned in regard to the mode of procuring
permits to fish in salmon rivers. This question was easily
answered until a recent decision was rendered by the Dominion Courts, affirming the riparian rights of the owners of
lands along the rivers.　Up to that time the control of all
salmon waters, as well above as below the flow of the tide,
was in the Dominion government; and the right to fish with
either seine or rod could only be obtained from the fishery
officials.　But now it is different.　Permits or leases can
only be obtained from the owners of the lands, whether such
ownership is in individuals or in the government.　Immediately this decision was rendered, gentlemen who were
promptly posted either took up the unentered government
lands commanding desirable pools, or secured leases from

It is generally believed that this decision will lead to the
early depletion of the now prolific rivers affected by it.　The
individual owners, even where they lease their pools, will not
be as likely to refrain from fishing them with either rod,
spear or net as when they were restrained by non-ownership or
through fear of the penalties of the old comprehensive and
rigorously enforced laws.　The government will, of course,
withdraw its guardianship from rivers from which it derives
no revenue.　To be sure, the individual owners or lessees
can appoint guardians, but it is very questionable whether
such appointees will be as careful or as efficient as those
who held an official commission.　The loyal residents on and

in the vicinity of the rivers have a profound respect for the authority of the Queen, even when that authority is represented by one of their own neighbors, but they have no more respect for individual rights, when those rights are simply guarded by those having no official authority, than our own free and independent citizens.

But I may be mistaken in regard to the effect of this change in the fishery laws of the Dominion. I certainly hope so; for it would be a great misfortune, not to the Provinces alone, nor yet simply to those who take delight in the princely sport of angling, but to all consumers of this kingly fish. For some reason yet unexplained, the salmon catch has largely diminished within the past few years. It would be a public calamity if this new policy should result in the indiscriminate slaughter of the whole salmon family while on their journey to and from their spawning beds at the sources of the rivers to which they resort to breed and multiply. I most sincerely hope that those who believe no harm will result from this change of policy are right. But I think otherwise, and believe my fears will be confirmed by a few years' experience.

This decision, it is proper to say, only affects the waters of Quebec and New Brunswick. Nova Scotia rivers, as I understand it, still remain open to all comers.

"Well," said one of my inquisitive friends, who has made up his mind to kill a salmon at any cost, "assume that, by hook or by crook, I have obtained a permit, what shall I do with it; or, rather, what must I do to render it available?"

"That is a question more easily answered than how to obtain a permit. The first thing needful is an appropriate equipment, such as rod, reel, flies and leaders. In regard to a rod, the essential things are strength and elasticity. Either can easily be obtained separately, but wood in which both are perfectly combined is hard to get hold of. But without both neither is of any use, either in casting or in killing. A rod that is unresponsive is not only a very unpleasant thing to handle, but will fail to do the work required even in the hands of an expert. No one can cast

a fly with a hoop pole, but one might almost as well have a
hoop pole as some rods that are palmed off as appropriate
for salmon casting. Unless the spring is equally distributed
from tip to butt, and can be distinctly felt at the latter as well as
clearly seen at the former, it is not a rod for the work for
which it is intended. But with such a rod casting is an absolute pleasure, whether the responses are few or many.
One may manage very well with an inferior line, if it only
has strength, with sec nd or third rate strong leaders, and
with flies which would not pass muster in the eye of an
artist, but he had better stay at home than to go to salmon
waters with anything less than a number one rod, whether
of wood or bamboo. My own favorite rod is of wood, but
it is fair to say that it is the only one of half a dozen that
can be branded as perfect. But this one is perfect. It has
the very spirit of elasticity in every fiber, and responds to
every movement as if instinct with life. Such a rod is
better than rubies, and is worth more than its weight in
gold. I would rather break every other rod I own than
raise so much as a splinter upon the surface of this grand
old hero of a hundred battles. Nevertheless, I have made
slightly longer casts with a bamboo, but I never give a large
fish its butt without a tremor. Its advantage is lightness of
weight—no mean advantage, be it understood, when one's
muscle is of delicate fiber.

"In fishing for salmon, I like a line of good weight—not
alone for strength, but for casting. A heavy eighteen-foot
rod needs something at the end of it you can feel. The
most accomplished expert would make poor work with a
light trout line on a double-handed salmon rod. An oiled
line of medium strand, a hundred or a hundred and twenty-
five yards in length, is what one needs. With such a rod
and line and with such leaders and flies—both in sufficient
numbers—as can be procured of any honest dealer, and a
reel made for use and not for ornament, one may feel sure
that good sport will not be marred by bad tackling."

"Thank you, so far; but after I have secured my tackling,
what am I to do with it?"

"My only reply to such a question is—use it."

"That's all very well; but how? Have you no specific advice to give a willing pupil on that head?"

"No; because while you may be taught by a cook-book how to dress a salad or stew a rabbit, I never knew an angler made by a written recipe. It is no more true that 'the proof of the pudding is in the eating' than that the only way to learn how to angle is to angle. One may be talked to until his head swims about fly-casting and salmon fishing and still make his first cast as awkwardly as if he had never seen a fly or stretched a leader. But those who have had any experience in casting for trout will have no difficulty in casting for salmon. The movements in both are practically the same. The only vital difference is in the weight of the rods, and this difference is practically neutralized by the fact that both hands instead of one are employed in the manipulation of the rod used in casting for salmon. During all my thirty years of exclusively trout or bass fishing I had never used a double-handed rod. When I first launched my canoe on a salmon river I had to float through a mile of water swarming with trout before I reached a pool where I could have an opportunity to cast for salmon. In making this distance I kept my eight-ounce trout rod in active motion, with such results as gave me a surfeit. When this stretch of water was passed, and my Indian gaffer said, 'Trout no more, salmon pool, trout rod no good,' I promptly, but very tremulously, took hold of my salmon rod, which looked ponderous as a weaver's beam and felt as heavy as a hemlock sapling, and prepared to reach out for the point indicated by my Indian mentor. Holding my rod in my left hand, with the butt pressed against my body, I pulled the line from the reel with my right hand, keeping it out by the required quick backward and forward movement until the desired length was obtained, when I seized the rod with both hands and found myself casting as easily and as steadily as if I had been 'to the manner born.' Although kind friends had given me a score of lessons, the memory of them had all vanished when the crucial moment came, but by simply doing, with a slight variation, what I had always done when casting for trout, I did just the right thing, in the right way, at the right moment. And when the rise came and I struck my fish, I did precisely what I would have done with a large trout or bass in similar waters. I held him taut when I could, gave him line when the pressure demanded it, reeled in when I could do so with safety, humored him when he sulked, brought him to within reach of the gaff as soon as possible, and landed him with a shout, probably the happiest man in all the Provinces. I have killed hundreds of salmon since, but I do not think I have ever cast better, manipulated my fish more discreetly, or received more deserved compliments from my critical gaffers, or heartier congratulations from my angling companions. No, a reasonably skillful trout fisher need have no fears about striking out boldly for salmon. It is only necessary for him to make careful use of what he already knows, and to take care that he does not 'lose his head' under the excitement of such sport as, in his wildest imaginings, he had never dreamed of."

"But," said a novice friend who is ambitious to graduate from a hand trawl to a fly rod, "what hope can I have to successfully tackle a salmon? Surely there are some rules a knowledge of which would assist such unfortunates as myself?"

"The only rule I can lay down for you and those like you who have the good sense to aspire to the dignity of salmon anglers is this: Begin as soon as you can and learn from experience. There is no other competent teacher. If you had an ambition to copy a Raphael, you might read every treatise that has ever been written on tone and tint, light and shade, the different varieties of color and the most effective mode of applying them, without being any the better qualified to make the copy than if you had never seen a Raphael. So it is with angling for salmon. No amount of reading or of mere verbal instruction, however clearly or graphically imparted, can give to you the rhythmic movement, the delicate twist, the careful manipulation, and the nice discrimination required to make a wise use of the constantly varying conditions in which an angler finds himself when casting for salmon.   Topsy wasn't brought up—she 'growed;' and that is the only way to become an expert on salmon waters.

"I never knew two anglers who cast exactly alike, while I have seen scores who were the peers of each other.   Each has his peculiar attitude, motion and swing; his straight, lateral or sweeping cast, but each reaches his goal with equal precision, if not with equal grace.   Each manipulates his fly on the water, awaits a rise, and strikes and fights his fish after his own fashion, but certain general principles are adhered to by all, and all have the same measure of felicity from the beginning to the end of the fray.   But whatever their manner of casting and striking and killing, the testimony of each will be, that whatever of skill they have was acquired, not from instructions in the theory of the art, but in the knowledge that came to them from actual experience; from all of which I do not wish to be understood as condemning the honest efforts of honest anglers to transform a novice into an expert by written or verbal instructions— I have done a little of both myself—but simply to impress the earnest aspirant with the fact that the only way to learn to cast is to cast, and the only way to appreciate the pleasure available to salmon anglers is to experience it.   As no man ever yet became acquainted with the luscious flavor of the creamy flakes of a well-cooked salmon by having some one glowingly describe how deliciously the delectable morsels rested upon his own gratified palate, so no man ever yet learned how to cast for salmon, or attained unto a full appreciation of the supreme delight wrapped up in the exercise and in the results which come from it, by being told how to do the one, or by having described to him the ecstacy of the other."

SALMON AND SEA TROUT HAUNTS AND HABITS.

In those vernal seasons of the year, when the air is calm and pleasant, it were an injury and sullenness against nature not to go out and see her riches, and partake of her rejoicing with Heaven and earth.— *Milton.*

Salmon are a dainty fish and never resort to streams which, in their normal condition, are turpid or impure. Like trout, they must have clear, cold water, where there are rocks and riffs and pebbly bottoms, and pools scooped out of the river bed and flanked by rapidly flowing currents. I never took a salmon in absolutely still water, and very seldom on shallow rapids. The former is not natural to them, and when in the latter they are pursuing their upward journey and are not easily diverted. They rest in pools, and there is where the angler looks for them and expects to find them, and when found and they are in the rising mood, no sport has ever yet been revealed to human consciousness which is more kingly.

The best trout streams are simply miniature salmon rivers. But trout are unlike salmon in their habits in this: In the early season trout are often found on riffs where the water is both shallow and rapid, but later on, from the middle of July to the close of August, no experienced angler would expect to find them there in any inviting numbers. In these hot months, when the water has become tepid, they resort to the mouths of cold brooks·or spring holes, and they need not be looked for elsewhere. But salmon are uniformly found, in August as well as in June, in pools. To be sure, when the water is well up, there are pools where there are only shallow riffs when the water is low. I have often taken fish at high water where I would. not think of casting for them when the water was low. Hence one never comes to know a river so as to make the most of it until he has fished it at all its stages. But whether the water is high or low it is all the same; salmon rest in pools, and it is the merest chance if any are taken elsewhere. In these pools the water is not always to say deep, but it is always of greater depth than the water in their immediate neighborhood, and the full force of the current is ordinarily deflected from them by the rocks of larger or smaller dimensions, whose position has given the motion to the water which, in time, has scooped out these resting places for the kingly fish.

On all the rivers I have fished for salmon—and I assume it be true of all others—the best pools are almost always found just above some rough or heavy rapid. The fatigue involved in ascending these rapids make rest all the more welcome. The excitement in fishing these pools is intensified by the doubt which always follows a strike whether you will be able to kill your fish within the limits of the pool or ·whether he will rush down the rapids, and so compel you .o follow him. In that case the chances are always against you, because, with all the skill of your canoemen, if you are in a canoe, or of yourself if you are on shore and the water renders wading possible, it is always questionable whether you can keep up with your flying fish. Besides, in rushing through a rapid full of rocks, there is always the chance that your line will get hitched, or, worst of all, that the fish may take it into his head to stop midway of the rapid, and thus, like a hunted deer, double on you and allow you to swoop past him, only to find out the fact when you have dropped into still water 'a hundred yards or more below the point where your fish is sulking. Under these latter conditions a hitched line is often the sequel; or, when it is

not, you can only force back your canoe against the impetu-
ous current to where your fish is sulking by the most her-
culean efforts. When that point is reached and you find
your line happily free, you can only hope that he will
start; and when he does start under such circumstances it is
almost invariably down stream, with a rush, and you after
him under such a pressure of excitement as renders you
equally indifferent to danger and unconscious of fatigue.
When the foot of the rapids is reached the fight is renewed,
but you are master of the situation if you have shown ordinary skill thus far, and it is only a question of time—if you
are well hooked—when the gaff will be called into requisi-
tion.

When you are casting from the shore and you are obliged
to follow your fish on foot through even shallow rapids,
you need to have all your wits about you, and to bring out
all the highest skill there is in you; first, to preserve your
footing upon the slippery rocks over which you must pass,
and secondly, to take care that your fish does not run faster
than you do yourself, and so get out more of your line than
you wish him to have. In this sort of fishing you have one
advantage over the canoe, you need not move faster than
your fish, and if he chooses to take a rest midway of the
rapid, so can you. But it is an unpleasant time for a fish to
sulk when you are waist-deep in the water awaiting his
pleasure. I have more than once stood thus an half hour at
a time, finding it impossible, by any skill at my command,
to start the stubborn brute. Once I was dragged to the foot
of a rapid which terminated in a deep hole, through which
there was no way of passing but by a plunge and a swim.
Of course, no one in such a contest would give up beat
when a cold bath gave promise of victory. The provoca-
tion in this particular case was that immediately after the
gamy fellow had compelled me to take this plunge he sur-
rendered—coming up to the gaff so soon as I could reach a
footing and give him the butt.

But these rapids tussles are glorious when the fish makes
a straight wake for the easily flowing water below them. It

is grand to stand up in your canoe when both fish and canoe
move at equal lightning pace, and you are able to keep a taut
line upon him every inch of the way. I have often had just
such experiences, and the recollection of them still stirs the
blood like the sound of a trumpet.

Sea trout show themselves wherever salmon are found, but
not always simultaneously with them. In rivers where the
salmon run begins in May or early June, you need not look for
sea trout in any considerable numbers before well on into July.
Intermediately they are found in tidewater at the mouths of
the salmon rivers, and often in such numbers and of such
weight as give the angler superb sport. Three, five and
seven pound fish are not uncommon, and I have heard of
them of even greater weight, but I have never myself taken
one of over five pounds—two poun ds less than a real brook
trout, I once killed in the Rangeley waters, a beautiful fac
simile of which was kindly painted for me by Dr. Otis, of
New York, who was in camp with me at the time. There
is no picture in my collection I value more highly.

Next to salmon fishing I know of no more exciting sport
than angling for sea trout in waters where they reach their
highest dimensions; for waters differ in regard to this fish
as in regard to both brook trout and salmon —the weight of
all fish being determined by the abundan ce and quality of
the feed available to them. There are salmon rivers open to
all comers for sea trout alone, after the salmon season is
over, say from the middle of September on. I can imagine
few things more fascinating than such an excursion. I
know a river that you can strike fifty miles above its mouth,
by an easy portage of six miles from the st eamboat landing.
To float down these fifty miles with the current, in a bark
canoe, with such scenery on either hand as can hardly be
excelled on the continent, is something which any appreciative angler might covet. It is a trip I have never yet
found leisure to take, but affairs will go hard with me if I do
not try it the coming season.

Like trout, salmon vary in size in different rivers. Why
this is so is a mystery which I have not been able to solve.

It cannot result from either the quantity or quality of food in the rivers, because it is assumed to be a settled fact that salmon are very light feeders—if they feed at all—in fresh water. Possibly the difference comes from the greater or less abundance of food found by the fish in their salt water rambles. Far-fetched as this conjecture may be deemed to be by those who are as ignorant of the subject as I am myself, it may, perhaps, after all, furnish the true solution; because, as the instincts of the fish always bring them back to the rivers where they were hatched, may not the same instinct keep them to their own feeding ranges when outside? If so, and if these ranges, like trout waters, vary in the kind and quality of food available, the fact will affect their weight. I simply state this as a hypothesis. If I am at fault, and if any one can solve the problem "by authority" or otherwise, I will be very glad to hear from him. Certain it is that those who have heard much about salmon rivers from those acquainted with them, have heard such phrases as these: "Yes, there are plenty of salmon in such a river, but they are small." In such another river we are told: "The fish are in moderate numbers and of fair size," and of others we are told: "The fish may not be as plenty as in some rivers, but they run large," and so on of rivers from one end of the coast to the other. In one where I have fished, a 35 pound salmon was not uncommon. The largest fish I ever landed weighed 39½ pounds, but I fought a fish for two hours which finally broke away and was taken next morning in a net nine miles below with my fly in his mouth, and he weighed 42 pounds. One gentleman, Mr. Spurr, of St. John, N. B., killed two 40 pound fish in the same river the preceding year. It was in this river, also, that General Arthur killed his famous 50 pound salmon, and where Mr. Dun, his companion, lost a fish after a long struggle, which immediately afterward floated into a net with the evidence of Mr. Dun's ownership in his mouth. This fish weighed 52 pounds.

These monsters were caught in the Cascapedia, a river in which forty fish that I took one season averaged 25¼ lbs., and five of these only weighed 11, 15, 17, 19 and 21 lbs. respectively. The Restigouche is almost equally famous for its large fish, and the Metapedia and Merimichi used to be. In the rivers I have more recently fished the average of a season's catch will not exceed 18 lbs., and the largest I ever caught in my present river weighed only a fraction over 29 lbs.

But I trust no reader will imbibe the idea from what I have written that the sport of salmon angling depends upon the size of the fish. As a rule there is more lightning in a 12 lb. than in a 35 lb. salmon, and I have had more trouble killing fish of the lesser than of the heavier weight. They don't fight so long, but they are vastly more lively while they are fighting. The only fish I ever found it impossible to prevent running under my canoe so as to do me damage weighed but 11 lbs. The movement smashed my rod into several pieces, and I only landed him after the exercise of such skill and patience as excited the wonder and admiration of my delighted gaffer, and astonished myself.

I cannot call to mind the record of any salmon taken with a fly on this side the water larger than that killed by Gen. Arthur. But larger fish are recorded as having been killed with the rod in English and Scotch waters. One was taken last summer in the Tweed that weighed 60 lbs. An English earl is credited with one that weighed 69¾ lbs. A Highlander, after an all-night fight, is said to have landed a 73-lb. fish, and Hofland says a salmon was sold in the London market which weighed 83 lbs. When this was, or how taken, is not stated. I know Christopher North once declared he had killed a fish weighing "90 lbs. neat." But I make no account of that fish, because it was only caught with "a long bow," to serve as a climax to the Ettrick Shepherd's extravagant "fish stories," as given in Mackenzie's edition of the "Noctes Ambrosianæ," vol. 4, p. 83, 84:

SHEPHERD.—What creel-fu's [of trout] you maun hae killed!

NORTH.—A hundred and thirty in one day in Loch Awe, James, as I hope to be saved—not one of them under—

SHEPHERD.—A dizzen pun'—and twa-thirds of them abune't. Athegither a ton.

NORTH.—* * * And poor Stevenson, mild and brave—now no more —with his own hands wreathed round my forehead a diadem of hetherbells and called me King of the Anglers.

SHEPHERD.—Poo! That was nae day's fishin' ava, man, in comparison to ane o' mine on St. Mary's Loch. To say naething aboot the count less sma' anes, twa hundred about a half a pun, ae hundred about a hail pun, fifty about twa pun, five-and-twenty about fowre pun, and the lave rinnin' frae half a stane up to a stane and a half, except about half a dizzen, aboon a' wecht, that put Geordie Gudefallow and Huntly Gordon to their mettle to carry them pechin' to Mount Benger on a han' barrow.

NORTH.—Well done, Ulysses!

SHEPHERD.—Anither day in the Megget I caucht a cart-fu'. As it gaed doon the road the kintry-folk thocht it was a cart-fu' o' herrius —for they were a' preceesely ae size to an unce—and though we left twa dizzen at this hoose—and fowre dizzen at that hoose—and a gross at Henderland—on coontin' them at hame in the kitchin, Leezy made them oot forty dizzen, and Girzzy forty-twa, aught; sae a dispute haen arisen, and of course a bet, we took the census ouer again, and may these be the last words I sall ever speak, gin they didna turn oot to be Fourty-Five!

And here is where Christopher's ninety pound salmon comes in:

NORTH.—The heaviest fish I ever killed was in the river Awe—ninety pound neat—I hooked him on a Saturday afternoon and I had small hopes of killing him, as I never break the Sabbath. But I am convinced that within the hour he came to know that he was in the hands of Christopher North, and his courage died. I gave him the butt so cruelly that in two hours he began to wallop, and at the end of three he lay dead at my feet, just as

"The star of Jove, so beautiful and large,"

tipped the crest of Cruachan.

SHEPHERD.—Hoo lang?

NORTH.—So beautifully proportioned, that like that of St. Peter's or St. Paul's you did not feel his mighty magnitude till after long contemplation. Then you indeed knew that he was a sublime fish, and could not but smile at the idea of any other salmon.

TICKLER.—Mr. De Quincey, now that these two old fools have got upon angling—

SHEPHERD.—Twa auld fules! You great, starin', Saracen-headed lang-shanks! If it werna for bringin' Mr. North intill trouble, by haen a dead man fund within his premeeses, deal tak me gin I wudna fractur' your skull wi' ane o' the cut crystals.

After reading this dialogue, no one will doubt that Christopher North's ninety pound salmon was killed with "a long bow" instead of a Jock Scott.

SEVERAL RELEVANT TOPICS.

Forced from their homes, a melancholy train.—*Goldsmith.*

I find the following paragraph in a fairly-written book, printed in England fifteen years ago, with this title, "Chiploquorgan; or, Life by the Camp Fire in Dominion of Canada and Newfoundland, by Richard Lewis Dashwood, XV. Regiment."

"We were much surprised and disappointed at the paucity of salmon on our way up the Cascapedia, and when we reached the Forks only succeeded in killing two after several day's fishing. We therefore came to the conclusion that the river as regards salmon was a myth, and decided to return to the sea."

This visit was made in July, 1862. "The Forks," where barely two salmon were killed, are about fifty miles from the mouth of the river, and "on his way up," Col. Dashwood and his companions passed a score of pools where I have killed many scores of salmon, and which no one now-a-days with any sort of skill could fish without being amply rewarded for the time and toil required to reach them.

The "paucity" experienced by this party in 1862 can not be attributed either to their want of proficiency or to their ignorance of the habits of the fish, for the Colonel was an old salmon angler, having fished all the best salmon waters of the "old country," and was accompanied by a gentleman as noted for his skill as for his eccentricities. Nor could their ill luck have resulted from their want of knowledge of the locality of the pools, for some of them are so conspicuous that any "wayfaring man, though a fool," could not have made a mistake.

To what then could this "paucity of salmon" in this long famous river be attributed? Making all due allowance for any want of skill or knowledge or application on the part of these gentlemen, I am inclined to attribute their disappointment to the fact that the salmon were not then in the river in any such numbers as they have been since, and for this reason:

Twenty years ago that river and all others were open to all comers, whether with net, rod or spear, and because of this fact it had not only been thinned out, but by the merciless way in which the fish were hunted in season and out of season—in the estuary, in the pools and on the spawning beds—they were given no opportunity to multiply. By this persistent slaughter, continued for years in all rivers accessible to the salmon purchaser and packer, the kingly fish in the lower Provinces would very soon have shared the fate of their predecessors in the Upper Canada waters and in our own rivers on the south shore of Lake Ontario and the St. Lawrence. For it is not simply from far-back tradition that we know that salmon were once abundant in these Lake Ontario tributaries. I have myself (when a lad) seen canoe loads of salmon brought into "Little York," now Toronto, by the Indians, who had captured them in the rivers "Humber" and "Credit" at the head of the lake.

A venerable gentleman of Keesville (Mr. Arnold, now deceased) once told me that in 1818, he had purchased a salmon freshly caught at Oswego for a "York shilling," and that for several years afterward they continued to be taken in great numbers in that neighborhood. And you may remember that Mr. Weed was moved by the recollections awakened by the account I gave of "my first salmon," to publish in the *Tribune* some years ago, the account of his capture of a salmon in Onondaga Creek, near the present site of the city of Syracuse. He then lived in that neighborhood. One night he observed the flashing of bright lights along the creek, and on going out to see what was up, he found a party of Indians with spears and clubs, killing salmon as they were trying to force their way over the shallows of that stream. It was then and there, borrowing a spear from a friendly Indian, he killed *his* first salmon. To us of to-day this fact seems incredible. Nevertheless, that incident was but one of a thousand like it occurring in the shallows and pools of all the streams which then made their way, unobstructed by milldams or other barriers, to the lake.

But for these obstructions, supplemented by choking saw-dust and poisonous chemicals, many of these streams would have continued to be what they once were, the chosen resorts and spawning beds of this favorite fish, whereas now, not a salmon, except at one or two points, where they have been or are being artificially propagated, is seen in any river between Montreal and Hamilton. I would not complain of this if it had been a square question between progressive industry and the extermination of the lordly salmon; but we now know that, in many rivers, their extermination was not neccessary to the development of industry. If the mill-dams had been constructed so that the fish could have sur-mounted them (as is easily practicable), salmon would have continued to ascend the streams, and would still be found in waters from whence they have been driven by the erection of these impassable barriers. Although the Dominion government is endeavoring to undo the mischief already done, I fear it will take many more years to replenish than it did to deplete these once prolific salmon waters.

A year or two before this developed "paucity" of the Cascapedia and other rivers of the lower Provinces, having learned by experience that it would be too late to lock the stable door after the horse was stolen, stringent laws were passed by Parliament to protect the fisheries in all waters under government control. But, unfortunately, while the original laws contained sundry useful provisions, they were fatally defective in that all persons were "forbidden to fish for, capture or kill fish by means of spears, except only the Indians." This exception rendered the law practically nugatory. The deadly spear had been the chief cause of all the mischief, and so long as this permission continued it would be impossible to bring the rivers (in the neighbor-hood of localities where the speared fish could be exchanged for rum and tobacco) back to their original status. This spearing clause was still in force in '62, when Col. Dash-wood made his trip up the Cascapedia, and to that fact may be attributed the then "paucity" of the river as he found it. Soon afterward, spearing even by Indians was strictly prohibited, and as a result the river became in a few years the most noted on the continent; and it will so continue, unless the recent riparian rights decision shall work as mischievously as many believe it will.

I made my first visit to the Cascapedia in '74. At that time the stringent fishery laws—including the prohibition against spearing by Indians as well as by all others—had been in force for eight or ten years, and, however it may have been before, it certainly was not then true that "the river as regards salmon was a myth." Its waters were teeming with the lordly fish, and their capture afforded all the excitement and sport any reasonable angler could desire. Whether at the "Sheddon Pool," ten miles, or at "the Forks," fifty miles above the mouth of the river, fish were found in satisfactory numbers. But I had other proof than that furnished by Col. Dashwood that it had not always been so. Mr. Best, an intelligent *habitant*, who occupies the last house on the river (ten miles from the bay), and who has lived on the river for thirty years, told me that the fish were never so abundant as they then were; that they were far more numerous than ten years previously, and were increasing in numbers every year. In asking him how he accounted for the increase, his response was, "A strict guardianship and no more spearing by anybody."

But something more is necessary to keep up the supply, even though the recent riparian decision shall not work the mischief apprehended. The nets at the mouths of the rivers should be raised for two or three instead of one day in the week, to enable a larger number of fish to reach their spawning beds. Now that every pool on every available river is persistently fished, a much larger percentage of immigration is necessary to keep up the supply. If this is not secured, even with the otherwise effective protective laws, there will be inevitably a rapid diminution of salmon available to either seine or fly.

But the sea-trout will remain, whatever may become of

the salmon; and they are next of kin to that noble fish in habit, weight, flavor, and every gamy quality.

Until within a very few years not many anglers on our side of the line were in the habit of "going for" salmon. Even so recently as ten years ago a "Yankee" was seldom seen on the best rivers. But they have of late multiplied twenty-fold, and if they do not now they soon will constitute a majority of the "simple wise men," to whom the gentle art has become irresistibly fascinating; and the fact is not altogether agreeable to our English cousins, whatever our Canadian neighbors may think of it. The London *Field* gives expression to its displeasure thus:

"The principal rivers are leased by Americans, to whom money is no object. When they take a fancy to a particular river, there is no mistake about it, they will have it."

And the *Field* only speaks the simple truth. The New York Club, of which President Arthur, Mr. Vanderbilt, Robert Dun and a score of other wealthy gentlemen are members, paid a fabulous price for the best portion of the Restigouche, and Mr. Blossom and his associates were almost equally liberal in the price they paid for the lower twelve miles of the Cascapedia. These are, by all odds, the best rivers in the Provinces. Other first-class rivers will be, if they have not already been, similarly secured "by Americans, to whom money is no object." And the opportunity to do so has been greatly facilitated by the recent riparian decisions. Previously, the government officials had supreme control, and they were not always indifferent to the solicitations of their home friends. Leases, like kisses, often went by favor, as more than one American bidder has had occasion to know. But individual owners are not likely to forego a good offer from a "Yankee" to accept a poorer one from a "Kanuck." The result will be a more equitable distribution of leases and permits and an increased influx of American anglers. So be it. Men who have money to spend for coveted enjoyments can expend it for nothing more healthful, harmless and exhilarating than in the delightful pastime of angling for salmon.

THE GAME LAWS—ANGLING MISHAPS—SEA AND BROOK TROUT.

He who has once experienced the fascination of the woods-life never escapes its enticement. In the memory nothing remains but its charm.—WARNER.

Our local coterie were in council a few evenings since, nominally to devise means to render such aid as was practicable to secure an amendment and more general enforcement of the existing game laws of the State, but really for a promiscuous confab upon the subject of angling in general. The game laws were conceded to be imperfect, but less so than the slip-shod way in which they were enforced. Every species of fish and game are ruthlessly pursued out of season and by prohibited devices. This is true not alone in regard to remote waters and ranges, but also in regard to lakes and streams in populous neighborhoods. And this state of things will continue until the general public shall reach a more just conception of the material value of well-stocked waters in all sections of the State. As a partial remedy, an increase of the number of game constables was suggested. The necessity for this is conceded by those in authority, and if, in addition, those who appreciate the importance of game protection shall exert their personal influence to secure a thorough enforcement of the law in their several localities, something effective might be accomplished. At a few points in the State there are organized associations, one of whose purposes is to prosecute offenders. Some of them have rendered good service, but they are not generally efficient. Their members are ordinarily busy men, who have no leisure to give personal attention to the frequent violations of the law by the poachers and pot-hunters of their neighborhoods. If these several organizations could or would, for a year or two, employ some one to give his entire time to the detection and prosecution of offenders, they would learn to fear if not to respect the law, and good results would follow.

Our own State is not an exception to the prevailing vandalism. Not only do these violators of the laws of nature and of man deem all game their rightful plunder, but they persist in bagging it at all seasons and by any device. This is as true on the vast plains of the great West as within the borders of civilization, and is as persistently practised on the recently stocked salmon waters of Maine as in the over-fished lakes and rivers of the Adirondacks. Public sentiment is being gradually educated up to the proper standard upon this subject and it will ultimately reach a point when it will serve as a moral check upon all classes of the community, but meanwhile nothing but the terrors of the law and the enforcement of its penalty will act as sufficient restraints upon its habitual and persistent violators.

"If all has not been done that is desirable," said one of our number, "something has certainly been accomplished by the discussion of this subject within the past twenty or thirty years. I remember when sportsmen—not professional poachers or pot-hunters—did not deem it unsportsmanlike to string set-lines in the lakes and rivers of the North Woods to swell their 'count.' This practise has, I believe, been generally discarded, except by the low-down riff-raff, who have no more idea of what is legitimate in the practise of the art than an Esquimau has of the principles of algebra.

"I once met one of these fellows on the North Branch of the Moose River a great many years ago. We saw him set his line at a point famous for the number and size of the trout, which seemed to make it their headquarters. He supposed himself unobserved, of course, and retired to his shanty sure of a good haul in the morning. I was in camp with Dick O., whom most of you knew as 'a fellow of infinite humor,' and as muscular as he was witty, and as fond of fair play in angling as he was 'down on' all poachers and pot-hunters. When it was suggested that we make a midnight raid upon the trap set by our neighbor, Dick dissented, with the remark that 'he would make him a visit early in the morning, give him due notice of his purpose, and cut his line before his eyes.' I offered to accompany him, but he declined my services and proceeded alone to perform his righteous office. I watched him on his mission, observed him talking to the poacher, and saw him stoop down at the edge of the water, as if to cut the line. A tussle followed, and in less than a minute 'something dropped' in the water, and it wasn't Dick. The issue was the capture of the set-line; and, after due explanations, apologies, and sundry soothing appliances, a treaty of peace was signed, Dick was forgiven, and the poacher promised 'never to do so no more.'"

"Was that the season I met you fishing under water?"

"'No more o' that, Hal, an' you love me.'"

"Why not? It was certainly nothing to your discredit, and I have had a many hearty laugh since, at the remembrance of it."

"Tell us about it, D."

"Well, it was something like this: I was wading and casting down the North Branch with results entirely satisfactory, when I reached the borders of a rather deep pool, into which the waters swept with a velocity which rendered it extremely difficult for me to keep my footing. Anxious to reach a shaded spot in the pool, which required a long cast, I lifted myself up upon a slippery boulder to the more certainly reach my objective point. I succeeded, as I expected, in raising a large fish, but in striking, my feet slipped from under me, and I glided into the flood as cleanly and as arrow-like as a saw log dips into the water below the chute. I was not aware that anyone was in the neighborhood, until I heard a roar of laughter as I emerged from my bath to swim ashore. That's the whole story; I saw nothing laughable in the adventure then, although I have often since smiled in thinking of it."

"No, gentlemen, that is not the whole story, begging my friend's pardon. After he made his plunge there was nothing to be seen of him or of his belongings, but his rod, and that was held as erect and as artistically as if he was playing his fish from the rock from which he had slipped. The line was kept taut, and the tip of the rod bent as gracefully while the angler was submerged as when he regained his footing. It was a fine illustration of the ruling passion, and I was as glad as if I had done it myself, when our friend landed a three-pound trout as the result of his judicious manipulation under difficulties. By the way, D., did you ever find your hat?"

"Yes, half a mile below, and none the worse for the journey, But since you have begun to 'tell tales out of school,' I have a mind to give you a Roland for your Oliver."

"Let's have it; let's have it," from all sides. "Bob will not object."

"Not I, for I am sure nothing can be said about my angling adventures which will not redound to my infinite credit."

"We had been leisurely floating down the Raquette on such a day as rendered one quite indifferent to any past or any coming event except the going down of the sun. It was just such a day as one would like to have last forever. As we floated, we cast hither and thither, from no special desire to get a rise, but simply that our well-balanced rods might share in the inexpressible felicity of those who wielded them. It was well on in the afternoon when we touched the head of the long rapids near the Oxbow—in old times one of the best points for large trout, and plenty of them, on the river. My friend here was the first to get a rise, and was doing his best to land him at the head of the pool. But the fish and the current combined were too strong for him, and while both guide and angler were more intent upon the fish than upon their surroundings, the boat floated sideways against a projecting treetop, and was upset in the twinkling of an eye. The water was rather more than shoulder deep; but before I could cross over to help him, my friend had reached terra firma, while the guide was swimming with the current to overtake his boat. It is proper to say that Bob kept his temper, although he lost his rod."

"I remember those rapids very well," said another of our

number, "but I have not visited them since the Raquette waters were planted with pickerel by a Long Lake vandal, whose name I have forgotten."

"But I haven't. It was Lysander Hall, who had often served as my guide, and an excellent guide he was—quick, intelligent, obliging and better acquainted with all the by-paths of the wilderness than any guide I ever had, except George Morse, who was killed in the war, and over whose remains Gen. Spinner caused to be erected a fitting record of his patriotism and courage."

"No matter what he was in all else, in thus polluting the Raquette waters, Hall committed a crime for which there was no law to mete out to him fitting punishment. The grandest trout waters in the State are deteriorated for all time. But, as I was saying, I remember those long rapids very pleasantly, and except at Setting Pole, I enjoyed swift water fishing nowhere else so well. Since I last visited them I have done something in the way of killing sea trout, and I seldom cast in the swift waters where they are found without being reminded of the rapids on the Raquette."

"Are not the fish even more alike than the waters they inhabit?"

"At first I thought the fish not only alike in appearance, but alike in fact. But I have since changed my opinion, and now believe them to be quite distinct from our brook or river trout, but of course, of the same general family."

"In this," I replied, "you are at odds with some of the best writers."

"I know that very well, but I know also that I am in agreement with others, and where doctors thus differ I have tried to decide for myself, not by any scientific investigation—although I have done a little of that—but by a close observation of the haunts and habits of the fish. Some of the salmon and sea trout rivers I have fished are fed by numerous small tributaries which are full of brook trout, and when coveting a mess, as we often did, I knew just where to find them. I have one special brook in my mind which projected its cold, pure transparent water into the river with such force as to preserve its identity for some distance. Whenever I cast within the radius of this distinctively marked brook water I would take clearly marked brook trout ranging from a quarter to half a pound, but if I cast beyond this line so much as a half dozen yards I would have no brook trout response. When the clearly defined river water line was reached, the dainty fish seemed to halt as surely as if they had run their heads against a stone wall. But, by extending my cast beyond the outflow of the brook, I would receive prompt responses from what I believed to be sea trout. On placing them side by side the difference in their appearance seemed to me to be something more than the difference caused by the difference of the water in the two streams. But both are beautiful fish, but, in such a side by side comparison, the sea trout is discovered to lack the rich lustre and golden beauty of his more dainty cousin."

"Just," I added, "as you will find the tiny fry you see in the little spring rivulets which empty into a trout lake to be more beautiful in form and color than the larger fish you find in the larger waters."

"It was long a question," my friend rejoined, "whether pickerel and muscalonge were not identical. Now we know that they are different fish, and yet they resemble each other quite as closely as sea and brook trout. Among all the trout I have taken in salmon waters I never saw one that bore an exact resemblance to the trout I have taken in real trout brook waters, or that leaped from the water to the fly with the same vim which distinguishes the large brook trout in our own northern lakes and rivers. I have no wish to be dogmatical upon this subject, but I shall hold to my opinion all the same."

"I do not care to argue the question with you," was my reply, "but I am not convinced. I agree with you in this, however, that, except salmon, I know of no fish that affords better sport to the appreciative angler than sea trout ranging from three to eight pounds in weight."

ODDS AND ENDS.

I would do what I pleased, and doing what I pleased, I should have my will; and having my will, I should be contented; and when one is contented there is no more to be desired; and when there is no more to be desired, there is an end of it.—*Cervantes.*

At a recent sitting of the local brotherhood, one of them was moved to murmur thus:

"My usually placid temper is often disturbed by the stupid criticisms which outside barbarians sometimes pronounce upon our gentle pastime. Their ignorance is their only excuse. But men have no business to speak dogmatically upon a subject of which they know nothing. And this is just the mental status of those who speak disparagingly of angling and of those who engage in it. There is a thousand times more of the divine element of saintliness in our harmless and healthful recreation than in the dirt-worm habit of perpetually delving for filthy lucre, and there is a great deal more of rock-bed common sense in a man who cheerfully spends ten dollars to preserve his health than in one who would rather jeopard his health than spend a dollar. No honest angler would ever wet a line if there were nothing in the art besides the mere material pleasure it affords him. But it has other and higher attractions— attractions which reach into the æsthetic realm and lift its votaries up to the very border-land of Bulah."

"We can all, I am sure," said another of our number, "speak from our own personal experience on this point. Two or three hours a day of the forty or fifty I pass on angling-waters every year, give me all the fishing I desire. The intervening time is filled up very delightfully in leisurely rambling through the silent woods; in reclining beneath some umbrageous arbor,

'Whose green leaves quiver with the cooling wind,
And make a checker'd shadow on the ground,'

and which overlooks the lake or stream on the borders of which I have pitched my tent; in clambering to the summit of some lofty eminence which gives me an enchanting view of the vast forests spread out illimitably before me; in floating hither and thither, where the kingly salmon

'Cuts with his flashing oars the silvery stream;'

in listening to the music of singing birds and to the melody of rippling waters; in lazily loitering about our cosy camp; in filling my exulting lungs with the pure atmosphere in which I am enveloped, and in inhaling the delectable odors of the virgin woods as they are borne to me by the summer zephyrs which sweep down from the forest-clad mountains with the refreshing balminess of the breath of the morning. Fishing is but a pleasant incident in these forest experiences. To me it simply gives zest to what, independently of it, is a source of perpetual delight.   Possibly, at first, I might not have sought out these quiet places if I had had no taste for angling; but certain it is that angling would never have come to be to me what it is if it had not been associated with, and if it were not a part of, these other and higher sources of mental and physical delights.   I am sure, also, that I am not exceptional either in my tastes or in my habits from the great mass of the brotherhood.   There is not a fluttering leaf, a rippling rapid, a silver cascade, a momentary sun-glint, a passing shadow, a bird note, a tiny flower, a feathery fern, or any one of a thousand other 'things of beauty' we see and hear where our pastime draws us, which is not remembered by the appreciative angler equally with the rise and strike and swirl of trout or salmon."

"That is true, every word of it," was the reply. "Angling never yet made a bad man worse, while it has made a great many good men better. I admit that all anglers are not saints, but I insist that they would be less saintly if they were not anglers.   For the recreation brings its votaries into close and constant contact with whatever is sublime and beautiful and exalting in nature, and no one can long hold communion and loving fellowship with the thing created without acquiring a higher appreciation of the beneficence, wisdom and power of its Creator."

"There is," I suggested, "one beautiful thing about angling which is well worth taking into account: one never wearies of it. Other pleasures grow stale or insipid, but this acquires new fascination with every new experience. This is the verdict of all who, 'e'en down to old age,' have secured mental rest and physical vigor from the practice of the gentle art, which good Sir Henry Wotton found to be 'rest to his mind, a cheerer of spirits, a diverter of sadness, a calmer of unquiet thoughts, a moderator of passions, a procurer of contentedness, begetting peace and patience in those who profess and practice it.'

"I have a friend who is the very type and embodiment of a happy angler and an honest man.

> 'Age sits with decent grace, upon his visage,
> And worthily becomes his silver locks;
> He wears the marks of many years well spent,
> Of virtue, truth well tried, and wise experience.'

"He has fished for fifty years, and is to-day even more eager to take his place on angling waters than when he first felt the ecstatic thrill which comes to all who have ever had the good fortune to kill a salmon. Here is what he says to me in a recent note:

"AT HOME, Dec. 12, 1882.

"*My dear D.:*

"What has become of you? Have you again been playing Cincinnatus on your Western ranch, or are you simply digging yourself out from beneath the political avalanche under which you and all of us were buried in November?

"As the hart panteth after the water brooks, so do I pant for the coming of the time of the singing of birds when it will be right to go a-fishing, where

> 'Soft whispers run along the leafy woods,
> And mountains whistle to the murmuring floods.'

"What a blessed time we shall have (D. V.) exploring the beautiful lakes mapped out for us by our faithful henchman, wherein no white man has ever yet cast a fly! I have 'dreams in the night' about them: for I know what they must be from what we have already seen of two of them. Husband your vitality, my dear fellow, that you may be able to make the circuit.

"Six months yet before the 20th of June! Meanwhile I will have passed my seventieth birthday, and as you, old chap, are 'there or thereabouts,' you cannot greatly boast over your humble servant. But, next to a vigorous youth commend me to a lusty old age and this is what both of us have had vouchsafed to us—for which devout thanks. But would it have been so but for the rest, recuperation and repose which have come to us from our annual visits to salmon waters?

"No politics in mine, if you please, for politics at present form no part of my mental ailment. I simply keep the run of things—feeling very much as Bret Harte's Abner Dean of 'The Society of the Stanislaus" felt:

'Then Abner Dean, of Angel's, raised a point of order, when
A chunk of old red sandstone struck him in the abdomen,
And he smiled a kind of sickly smile, and curled up on the floor,
And the subsequent proceedings interested him no more.'

"As ever and forever, yours,   H."

"The lakes referred to in the foregoing note are trout lakes in the vicinity of the salmon river myself and friend annually visit. We had heard of them but could find no one who had ever visited all of them. Last summer we requested our local servitor to hunt them up and make a map of them. This he has done, and I anticipate as much pleasure in visiting them as I do in fishing our favorite pools for salmon—not alone because we are sure to find them full of trout, but because we have found the two or three of the group we have already seen perfect gems of beauty. From my very first visit to the woods I have had a passion to hunt up new places, and make side excursions whenever I could hear of anything worth visiting. To do so often involved hard work, but that fact simply added to the fascination of the habit, and, I am inclined to believe, has contributed to the large measure of vigor which has continued with me through all these decades. Now that I have reached my three-score years and ten, I may not be able to pass over rough places or climb steep hills as sprightly as in the long ago, but I can do both passably well still, and find no abatement in the delight these adventures and the pleasant places they reveal afford me. Indeed, I am not sure that my fondness for them has not even outrun my passion for the excitement derived from the more material incidents connected with angling. Of this, however, I am sure, that every new exploration reveals to me new beauties; that many pretty bits of scenery that in my former greater haste were passed by unnoticed, now attract my attention and excite my admiration. Whether this is because we become more observant as we advance in years, or because our tastes, like our virtues and our vices, grow by what they feed upon, I cannot say. But this I know, that 1 look forward to no phase of the pastime with more glowing anticipation than to these delightful rambles."

"I notice," said one of our coterie, "that you speak of yourself and friend in a way that leaves the impression that you two make up your entire party in these annual excursions. Is that so?"

"Yes, not because we are unsociable or exclusive, but because we have both been taught by experience that the fewer cogs the less friction. I have known the start of a party of five or six delayed for a week because some one of the number was not quite ready; and not infrequently the equanimity of a whole camp is disturbed because some one wishes to go when others do not, or to stay when others wish to 'fold up their tents, like the Arabs, and silent steal away.' In a crowd, some are night birds, who never care to 'go home 'till morning,' or to bed either, while others deem sleep and regular hours as necessary to comfort in the woods as at home. Both classes may enjoy themselves equally well, but, though they may not say so, each in their hearts wish "tother dear charmers away.' It is best, therefore, when it can be done, that only those whose temperaments and home habits are similar should camp together, that as little as possible should interpose to mar the pleasure of these forest visits. My first experiences were in crowds. Later on, the number of my angling companions was gradually curtailed, until, during recent years, two of us, whose ideas of comfort and of times and seasons are always in harmony, constitute a 'party' as happy and contented as 'two drops of water blended into one.' "

"But," said my questioner, "how do you manage to pass the evenings? You must get talked out after a while, with only two of you to contribute to the common stock."

"That would be true if my friend was like some fellows I

know, who are really 'talked out' before they begin to talk at all, because they never have anything either useful or edifying to say."

"That's all very well, but for my part, when I am in the woods I don't care to be very 'edifying' myself nor to be very greatly edified by others, if by 'edifying' you mean only such conversation as would be expected from a party of monks in a cloister or of a bevy of savans in a salon."

"Nor do I, for I don't go to the woods myself to be superlatively grave, but to be innocently happy. My companion is *au fait* in all the intricacies of the law, in all the mysteries of the sciences, and, like all the graduates of Old Union when its historical President was at its head, he is as profound in the classics as he is familiar with current events. There is no subject about which he cannot converse—gravely, if the subject demands it, or humorously if otherwise. And as for myself, ask him, and if his friendship does not induce him to hide my faults, he will tell you that, while lounging around our camp-fire, I talk 'an infinite deal of nonsense; more than any man in all Venice.' No; there is neither wearisome sameness nor somnolent gravity in our party of two during the restful hours between early gloaming and our night retreat. If our conversation is not always what would please a fool if it is never what would disgust a scholar."

"I can very well believe that; but it has always seemed to me that at least a third party is necessary to give piquancy to personal jests; for how can one laugh at his own joke, or how can the other fellow be expected to laugh when he is its subject. A looker on in such an encounter is a mighty stimulant to one's wit."

"As to that, we are never without subjects that provoke laughter; but we always find it pleasanter to laugh with than at each other. He is walking on thin ice and making a dangerous experiment with assumed friendship who habitually indulges in either personal or practical jokes. He must be something more than a saint who always receives them with equanimity, and he a great deal worse

than an average sinner who, having a giant's strength in
that direction, persistently uses it like a giant. No 'practical joker' ever long retains the hearty respect of his friends,
nor their hearty friendship either. A persistent punster is
less offensive. He is only a bore; the other fellow is a nuis-
ance."

"Talking of practical jokes, "you remember the 'good
thing' played on Mark Antony when he was fishing with
Cleopatra:

> *Charmion*—" 'Twas merry when
> You wager'd on your angling; when your diver
> Did hang a salt-fish on his hook, which he
> With fervency drew up."

" 'Tony must have been in a sweet-tempered mood just
then to have received the joke complacently. I once knew
a miserly sort of a fellow who would almost literally sleep
on the brink of the best 'spring-hole' within a five miles'
circuit, in order to retain its monopoly. To punish him
for his unsportsmanlike behavior, one of the guides was
bribed to launch a hemlock bush upon the current every
two minutes, at a point just above the coveted spring-hole;
and while the astonished angler went up stream to investi-
gate, another chap took possession and held it through the
day. When told of the joke, instead of enjoying it he was
very angry, and I doubt whether he had a hearty laugh in
a twelve-month."

"The danger of practical jokes," I interposed, "is that
they are generally aimed at the most vulnerable point in the
victim's harness. For this reason, as in the case just cited,
they cut, because they are somehow felt to be deserved. A
proverbially thrifty chap would not feel half so much
offended by being presented with the empty shell of a
sucked egg as would a spendthrift who had 'wasted his sub-
stance in riotous living.' "

"You remember the case of ———" our practical joker
had begun to remark, when he was interrupted by the most
exemplary of our number, who said to him:

"Now, Jeemes, my good fellow, I see what you are

driving at.   You know only too well how you always fasci-
nate me when you draw your long bow, and you know just
as well that my time is up; and yet you are deliberately and
with coldly concocted malice, trying to beguile me into for-
getfulness and thereby subject me to a 'curtain lecture' when
I get home.   But you can't play any such practical joke on
me any more then you could humbug me by telling me I
was hitched to a log when I felt the twitch of a salmon.
So, 'go to' old man, and good night to all of you."